No School Left Behind

Books of Related Interest

Handbook on Effective Instructional Strategies: Evidence for Decision-Making
Myles I. Friedman and Steven P. Fisher

Ensuring Student Success: A Handbook of Evidence-Based Strategies
Myles I. Friedman

Educators' Handbook on Effective Testing
*Myles I. Friedman, Charles W. Hatch, Jacqueline E. Jacobs,
Aileen C. Lau-Dickinson, Amanda B. Nickerson, and
Katherine C. Schnepel*

No School Left Behind

How to Increase
Student Achievement

Myles I. Friedman

EDIE

THE INSTITUTE FOR EVIDENCE-BASED
DECISION-MAKING IN EDUCATION, INC.

Library of Congress Control Number: 2004115608
ISBN: 0-9666588-3-3

First published in 2005

The Institute for Evidence-Based Decision-Making in Education, Inc.
A South Carolina non-profit corporation
P.O. Box 122, Columbia, SC 29202

Printed in the United States of America

The paper used in this book complies with the
Permanent Paper Standard issued by the National
Information Standards Organization (Z39.48–1984).

10   9   8   7   6   5   4   3   2   1

To all who help improve our children's education

Contents

Acknowledgments

I want to thank Dr. Anne Bryant, Executive Director of the National School Boards Association, Dr. Pamela J. Grotz, Executive Director of the National Parent Teacher Association, and Renata Witte, a member of the National Board of Directors of the Parent Teacher Association, for their contributions to the development of this book. I also want to thank Drs. John King, Marvin Efron, Charles Hatch, and Mimi Maddock for critiquing the manuscript, and Meredith Fine for her contribution to the writing of this book. Finally, I am grateful to Betty Friedman for contributing to this book and preparing the manuscript.

1

Overcoming Obstacles

We, the people, are endowed with the responsibility of overseeing the education of America's children. Despite the support the public gives to education, serious problems remain. The purpose of this book is to renew optimism for the future of education by providing people who are not trained to analyze research with the scientific facts they need to improve our schools and elevate student achievement. Many parents, school board members, educators, politicians, and other citizens who affect education need to know what works in education based on solid research evidence. Let us begin by considering obstacles to progress as a basis for understanding the remedies presented in the coming chapters. (Supportive research is summarized in Chapter 9.)

One day in the late spring, the postal carrier brings you an envelope from your child's middle school. Inside is her report card: two "B's," an "A," and a "C." Next to each grade is a brief comment from most, but not all, of her teachers. "Could do better"; "Excellent book report"; "Lacks initiative."

What are you to make of this report card? Is Beth a good student, a mediocre one, or teetering on the verge of failure? The report card is practically useless in helping you make that judgment. The grades themselves are meaningless since the teachers have not made clear what standards underlie them. The teachers' comments are vague, subjective, and equally meaningless. The report card itself is too late to correct the problems in the social studies class where Beth got a "C." Meanwhile, Beth gets promoted to the eighth grade, without any assurances that she has actually mastered the material in seventh grade.

You make an appointment to speak with the teacher. He explains to you that in the course of an average day he has very little time to give individual students the help they need. He spends most of his time teaching the class, collecting permission slips, herding the class to assemblies, standing guard in the cafeteria at lunchtime, and trying to manage the two or three children in the class who are disruptive. In the evening he stays up late preparing the next day's lesson plan to make the most of his teaching time. He is frustrated and exhausted. He finds your child likable and compliant but has not had enough time to fully diagnose and work with her on her weaknesses.

Let's say you find yourself so motivated to improve education that you decide to run for your local school board. You spend three months meeting voters, speaking at debates, sending out mailings, and shaking hands. Somewhat to your surprise, you win. You find yourself with a $20 million budget, a defensive teachers' union, a hidebound administration, litigious parents, and tough new federal and state standards. The board itself spends more time deliberating brick-and-mortar and administrative decisions than on reforming instruction. To have an impact on the solution you need to view the realities of the problem.

Despite all the money and effort that has been poured into education reform across the country, these scenarios remain all too common. America has zero tolerance for drugs and violence but all too much tolerance for academic failure. Since 1983, when the National Commission on Excellence in Education published the landmark study *A Nation at Risk*, billions of dollars and incalculable time and energy have been spent on improving the public schools. Yet, today, there are far too many young people leaving school unprepared for college, work, parenthood, and citizenship.

If American schools were inefficient but still were preparing young people to succeed in the job market and family life, perhaps their failings might be bearable. But tens of thousands of young people enter adulthood without mastering the skills and information they need to succeed. Numerous efforts at reform have made little dent in the problem, largely because people are addressing symptoms rather than root causes. For instance, the recent national push for accountability testing does not increase academic achievement in and of itself; it merely prevents students who have not achieved grade-level objectives from being promoted. This country can do better. As a community, we can pinpoint problems and provide effective, research-based solutions.

Failing to fix the education system carries a high cost. Our tolerance for failure results in lost opportunities for individuals, waste for the nation's economy, and an unraveling social fabric. Up to 15 percent of students drop out of high school before graduating, and fully one-third of the country's 18-year-olds do not have a diploma. Many of those who do graduate lack the basic math and literacy skills needed in the modern workplace. In 1995, 29 percent of college freshmen were enrolled in remedial reading, writing, and math courses. Many businesses find that they must train new employees in basic writing and math skills. By our estimate, a staggering 80 million Americans are undereducated. If 80 million Americans were afflicted with a physical disease, the response would be swift and sure, but this disease has been allowed to fester.

The effects of inadequate instruction are not merely felt by individuals, but also by the country as whole. In a study of quality-of-life factors (Rosier & Keeves, 1991), the United States ranked thirteenth, behind such countries as Switzerland (first), the United Kingdom (second), Canada (sixth), Austria (seventh), Australia (ninth), and Sweden (tenth). The quality-of-life indicators showed that while America got high marks for its economic output, it got low marks for adult literacy, infant mortality, and the number of children in the workforce. It ranked fourteenth in political rights and tenth in civil liberties. These rankings relate directly to the education level of America's citizens. More recently, in November 2002, *USA Today* reported on a UNICEF study in which American schools ranked eighteenth among the world's 24 richest nations. The five most effective educational systems were in South Korea, Japan, Finland, Canada, and Australia.

For two decades, attempts to fix education have been scattershot and unsuccessful. Some parents have been driven to home schooling their children. But abandoning the public schools is not the answer to the problems of the larger society. Unlike schools in other countries, America's schools are committed to educating all children, regardless of personal or economic differences. This noble goal has been elusive, though, as school officials, parents, and elected officials too often rely on unproved theories and discredited methods. In addition, the public schools have been burdened by numerous initiatives and mandates that have nothing to do with education. Politics—local and national—and bureaucratic red tape deaden initiative and interfere with instruction. There are many conscientious and capable teachers in our schools. But they are no longer in control of their classrooms, and they are inundated with busy work that detracts from their teaching.

One of the most prevalent and disturbing problems in American schools is the continued practice of social promotion, pushing youngsters through school who have not met educational standards and without assurances that they are actually literate in language arts and math. There are no records of social promotions, but the number of semiliterate and illiterate job applicants implies that students are still being promoted to the next grade without mastering required learning objectives. Social promotion affects individuals by misrepresenting their achievement, creating and perpetuating a sense of inferiority. Sometimes these students are promoted because of pressure from parents, sometimes out of a misguided effort to boost self-esteem. Nothing could be more harmful to self-esteem, though, than knowing you can't read or do basic math. Students who are promoted without mastering material end up falling farther and farther behind in school, and many eventually drop out. If they do manage to stay in school, they graduate with a diploma that is worthless and a future that is bleak. The damage to individuals and the cost to society are incalculable. Social promotion warps the entire educational system and causes severe emotional damage to young people.

In fairness, educators have long struggled with ways to assure success for each child, and taxpayers have willingly spent tens of billions of dollars in that effort. Too often, though, decision-makers choose programs or approaches that are not based on solid research. They fall victim to fads or sales pitches that promise easy solutions.

Here are several ill-conceived approaches to solving the education crisis that may sound familiar:

SMALL CLASS SIZES

One common misconception is that class sizes are too large. Reducing class size is more efficient for teachers, but not students. Classes are easier to manage, to be sure, but there is no proof that achievement increases as a result. There are a number of studies on student/teacher ratios showing that reducing class size from 30 to 15 students per teacher is of little consequence. Research does show that class sizes must be lower than 15 students per teacher to dramatically improve performance, a ratio that is too expensive for most school districts to maintain. But classes of more than 15 students should not hinder learning if the teaching technique is correct and students receive all the instruction they need.

ABILITY GROUPING

For 70 years, pupils have been labeled by their perceived abilities. Once students are sorted out by ability, often through a standardized test, their classes and the course of their lives are largely predetermined. For example, students in "honors" classes are usually expected to advance to a four-year college program from high school and may receive preferential preparation; students in the general program might go to a community college after high school or they might go straight to work; and students in the vocational track essentially go right to work in high school, learning a craft or occupation.

Students in the honors or vocational tracks at least have a sense of clarity about their future, but the bulge of students in the general track too often get lost. Beth, for instance, with her two "B's," her "A," and her "C," is a perfect candidate for invisibility. She is quiet in class and, though interested in drama, is too shy to try out for the school play. She received her "A" in English, and her teacher has recommended her for honors English in eighth grade, but because the rest of her schedule is in the general track, only "regular," non-honors English is available to her. She doesn't think to complain, and no one tells you, her parent, that she should be in honors English.

There is no scientific basis for ability grouping, except in a few specific areas, such as enrichment programs for high-achieving students. But these minor gains are more than offset by the problems with grouping. Too often, teachers set their expectations to ability level and grade accordingly. Studies have shown that students will perform to the level of expectation, and that grades are often based on teachers' preconceived ideas of students' abilities.

The grouping of students of varying abilities, called heterogeneous grouping, actually helps most students; learning is reinforced when the brighter students help those who are struggling. If Beth were in a heterogeneous social studies class, the teacher might ask a high-achieving student to help Beth with a special project on ancient Greece, or the teacher might arrange for Beth to be tutored a few hours a week. The expectations on Beth in a heterogeneous class would be higher than if she were placed in a class of students deemed unworthy of a four-year college.

REINFORCEMENT

Rewarding desired behavior in lower animals, such as lab rats, in order to promote that behavior has long been a staple experiment among psychologists and other scientists, but that same theory does not work for academic learning. Humans are not robots who can or should be trained to push a lever in exchange for food. And in the classroom setting, what would constitute a useful reward? Food is too messy and money is unethical. In a classroom of, say, 20 children, how can one teacher possibly offer an adequate amount of reinforcement to each child?

Reinforcement shouldn't be confused with complimenting effort and achievement and providing feedback, each of which has a distinct and useful place in the classroom. Compliments and feedback are specific tactics for encouraging students to undertake the next lessons with confidence and enthusiasm. Reinforcement is a repeated attempt to use rewards to shape behavior. Research shows that reinforcement does not increase academic achievement.

WHOLE LANGUAGE INSTRUCTION

Still popular throughout the country, whole language instruction focuses on teaching children to understand concepts rather than individual tasks or skills. For instance, students reading a book would be expected to discuss the plot rather than learn how the story line was constructed and executed. Here's another way of looking at whole language: Think of a chocolate cake. There are different ways to learn about the cake: to study the final product, or in addition, to understand the recipe and how the cake was created. By understanding the relationship of the recipe ingredients and how they are combined, a student learns much more about the cake, and baking in general, than merely by savoring the end result.

Despite the lack of evidence supporting whole language instruction, this philosophy remains in widespread use for teaching reading, writing, speaking, and listening skills. Put plainly, the whole language approach does not work. This method is not a true technique in the sense of an incremental progression of skill sequences, but rather it is a fuzzy, ill-defined approach that may actually impede learning. It emphasizes context over correct usage. Children are moved from oral to written language using words they already know and without regard to proper spelling or grammar; in fact, students sometimes are encouraged to invent spellings. The interdependence of speaking, writing, reading, and listening is stressed at the expense of understanding individual words or thoroughly mastering one skill, such as writing. If a student fails to understand the meaning of a paragraph or a story, he is not taught to infer the meaning from understanding the letters, words, and punctuation.

While there is some slight evidence that whole language instruction can be useful in kindergarten, it actually seems to impair education for older children.

TEACHER CHARACTERISTICS

Teaching skills more than personal traits have been shown to increase student achievement. Some believe that a teacher's personality affects his or her competence—that teachers who are warm and amusing are better than those who are not. There is simply no evidence to support this belief. Such teachers may be a hit with parents and administrators, but personality bears no relationship to competence. Furthermore, teachers need not have an encyclopedic knowledge of a wide variety of subjects; they only need to have mastered the subjects they are teaching. Humorous anecdotes and sweeping intellect may be welcome attributes elsewhere, but in the classroom there is no substitute for excellent teaching skills. Just as most students can master material, more teachers can be effective if given proper training and supervision.

SCHOOL VIOLENCE

Another widely misunderstood obstacle to success is the role of violence in America's schools. There is a popular notion that classrooms and schools are awash in aggressive students. This is simply not true. In fact, a U.S. Department of Justice study shows that young people are far less likely to be victims of violent crime at school than they are away from school. Furthermore, violent crimes have declined in schools over the past 10 years, despite sensational media reports that imply otherwise.

SCHOOL BUILDINGS

Another myth is that new school buildings improve the quality of education in that building. In 1999, the U.S. Census Bureau reported that $18.7 billion was spent annually on school buildings, or $5,656 per pupil. A recent Government Accounting Office (GAO) report estimated that another $112 billion is needed to bring the nation's schools up to date. The GAO says about one-third of all public schools need extensive repair or replacement. For all of this investment, though, achievement scores have not risen to keep pace. There is simply no correlation between physical surroundings and academic success.

Look around the world. Children in foreign countries, such as European countries, have no trouble learning in buildings that are old; in many of these countries, academic achievement is higher than in the United States, yet they spend a fraction of what America spends on brick and mortar.

In Beth's hometown, voters recently approved $5 million to build a new elementary school. The current elementary school, circa 1968, is solid and there is no growth in the neighborhood student population, but the School Board felt it was out of date. Renovating the building for new technology and repairing the heating and electrical systems was much less expensive but was considered an inadequate band-aid solution, and there weren't enough athletic fields or parking spaces for visitors.

None of these problems relates to how well teachers teach and how well students learn, however. The money spent for a new building could have been used for true academic purposes, such as tutoring or more teacher training.

If a student's physical surroundings were truly inadequate—if every rainstorm brought buckets of water through the ceiling or the bathrooms didn't work—one would expect academic achievement to suffer. But in most cases, the focus on school buildings satisfies the needs of educational leaders who promote and take credit for them more than those of children. Of course, new buildings are needed to accommodate student population growth.

INCREASING ACHIEVEMENT

Young people need us to peel off layers of bureaucracy and social programming to reveal the heart of the education system: teaching and learning. The focus of this book is on increasing academic achievement. As we will discuss in Chapter 3, the most direct and potent approach to improving academic achievement is to improve instruction, both in the classroom and with extra support, such as tutoring. Research shows that students who receive all the instruction they need to master academic material will almost always be successful. Improving the quantity and quality of instruction must become the mandatory task of the country's education leaders.

More money isn't the answer. School officials have spent billions, yet student achievement has not followed. Although there is always a shortage of funds, sufficient money is available to increase student achievement. Money is simply being spent in the wrong places. Instead of new buildings, school districts need to provide more and better instruction.

ACCOUNTABILITY TESTING

The No Child Left Behind Act, passed by Congress in 2002, and similar acts passed by more than 40 state legislatures, establish accountability testing as a way to certify that students have met minimum standards for promotion. This could be done in as little as six hours simply by using well-established, commercially available achievement tests that assess all the subjects commonly taught across the United States. Students would be required to achieve minimum test scores to be promoted. This would stop social promotion and stem the flow of illiterate and semiliterate youth now flooding the job market.

Unfortunately, many states have engaged in accountability testing overkill, to the detriment of students, teachers, school administrators, and parents. States have entered into the test construction business full-scale, attempting to assess everything taught in the state. Testing has become much more rigorous which, consequently, increases the failure rate. In the many states that have raised test standards for promotion above the minimum, the failure rate is even higher. As a result, a rebellious coalition of angry parents and educators is emerging in great numbers—the teachers of students who fail and parents whose children have failed and had been promoted routinely in the past.

Educators who are now held accountable for their students' achievement are up in arms, attacking the powers responsible for accountability testing. Well-intentioned accountability testing is becoming a tragic mess in some states. Let's hope that sometime soon wisdom presides over academic assessment, social promotion is curtailed, and students and educators are not dubbed failures unnecessarily. (Details on testing are provided in Chapter 8.)

Accountability is a genuine problem. Unlike unsuccessful businesses, which disappear eventually, unsuccessful schools remain open. Parents, politicians, teachers, and alumni have a long list of excuses when students fail these tests. They argue that the tests aren't a good measure of achievement, that test scores were low because of the number of low-income or special needs students who took the test, that deteriorating buildings interfere with learning, that there are not enough teachers, that there are too many disruptive students in the class, that parents are insufficiently supportive, or that more money is needed. All of these complaints are symptoms of the problem, but they avoid directly addressing the problem itself: far too many students fail to achieve instructional objectives. School systems brag about star faculty, student awards, and exceptional facilities. It's time for them to take credit for reducing the failure rate.

American educators must resist those who want to use schools extensively for nonacademic purposes. These educators must break out of their traditional methods that have been inadequate. They must focus on improving instruction. With the proper teaching techniques and targeted resources, almost all students are capable of meeting minimum high school graduation requirements.

Too many educational decisions are based on sales pitches, political pressure, and bureaucratic regulations, instead of on scientific research. Even those educators who are aware of relevant research often don't understand how to interpret and use information. There is also a huge gap between researchers and practitioners, and much research is not presented in a practical, useful way.

But there is a wealth of research about education that is scientifically rigorous and important. This body of research shows that certain instructional techniques described in Chapter 3 can effectively increase student achievement. These techniques include a process called corrective instruction, whereby students are taught and quizzed until the teacher is assured that they have mastered an instructional unit.

While it is sometimes necessary for teachers to work with a classroom as a whole, the best method of teaching is one on one, where each student is taught individually. Research shows that one-on-one tutoring is the single most effective method of increasing academic achievement. There are numerous ways to approach tutoring, from low-cost alternatives to full-blown tutoring centers, but the key is to provide tutoring at convenient times and for all subjects, as outlined in Chapter 5. In addition, the UNICEF study mentioned earlier in the chapter reemphasizes the value of family support for student achievement. Involvement in tutoring is a key avenue for family support.

Current teaching and testing practices breed a dark swamp of low self-esteem. Students who are consistently branded "failures" fall farther and farther behind. Many sit quietly in class, hoping to be ignored. Those who are forced to repeat a grade find themselves in an alien and unwelcoming class. Some become disciplinary problems or drop out of school entirely. In a throwaway society that values immediate success and gratification, students who struggle are quickly abandoned. But with a system of corrective instruction and supportive tutoring, it is simply assumed that most students do not master material on the first try; instead, they are encouraged to continue, and they are constantly assured that they will receive all the instruction they need.

How would this system work? In the case of young Beth, her social studies teacher would have seen by October that she had not mastered elements of her social studies course. The teacher might have asked Beth to do a special project and to retake a test. If Beth still had not mastered the material, the teacher might have recommended her for tutoring. A trained tutor would work with Beth for two hours a week until Beth understood the lesson and was ready to move on.

Children are born with a hunger for learning. But that hunger to learn in school eventually dissipates by the time most children get to middle school. Teachers, too, are frustrated with the current system. People who chose teaching because they loved the idea of preparing the next generation are driven from their profession by red tape and politics. They have lost more and more control over instruction, which has been replaced by state-required procedures and textbooks; they are even discouraged from any kind of warm, personal relationship with their pupils because of litigation.

Instead of herding students from grade to grade, instead of leeching the joy from teaching, instead of sending half-literate young people into the world, American education must improve. It's time to move from the outskirts to the heart of the matter. Educational administration, school buildings, counseling, busing, parent support, public relations, and other factors may be essential to the operation of a school system—but **instruction** is primarily responsible for desired learning. Education will have reached its potential when all students are given all the instruction they need to master all learning objectives through high school. This book presents a blueprint that provides hope and opportunity for every student. Prescriptions for raising student achievement follow. Chapter 9 presents key research findings in plain English that support the prescriptions and lays a foundation for the gateway initiatives described in Chapter 10, initiatives that can begin immediately.

HIGHLIGHTS

To increase student achievement, it is necessary to discontinue common practices that don't work; for example, student reinforcement regimens, whole language instruction, reducing class size to 15 or above, and ability grouping. Proven teaching skills rather than personal traits must be the focus of teacher recruitment and preparation. Less money needs to be spent on brick and mortar and more on improving the quantity and quality of instruction, including tutoring. Accountability testing must be refined and accountability overkill must be curbed.

2

A New Beginning

Jorge is about to turn 5. He is a bright-eyed, happy child who has spent the past year in a preschool program. He is able to get himself ready for school in the morning, he knows the alphabet, and he understands disciplinary rules, but he has some trouble with his coordination. Is Jorge ready for kindergarten or does he need another year of preschool?

One of the most stressful moments in the life of a young parent is the first placement test: Is my child ready for kindergarten? Parents have good reason to pay attention. The readiness test is, in fact, important. It judges a variety of student abilities and screens for developmental or physical impairments. (Commonly used early childhood readiness tests are mentioned in Chapter 8.) An accurate placement can set a child on a solid course for success and, conversely, an inaccurate placement can cause a child endless frustration. But parents often set the wrong standard for success. The goal is not placing a child into kindergarten; the goal is to place the child where he can flourish.

Schools should not rely on one test to assess a child's readiness for school; rather, they should attempt to get a comprehensive, in-depth understanding of a child. A simple questionnaire is inadequate. Good testing should reveal the following information:

- Self-help readiness, including eating, toileting, dressing, and other self-care skills;
- Psychosocial readiness, including following adults' instructions, cooperating with peers, knowing social rules, and not presenting a physical danger to themselves or others;

- Language readiness, including visual and hearing skills, speaking, comprehending stories, and identifying body parts, colors, objects, actions, letters, sounds, and numbers;
- Motor coordination readiness, including both small and large movement capabilities; and
- Thinking readiness, including understanding relationships, causality, and consequences.

The assessment should show whether a child is delayed, normal, or advanced for his age group. It should also provide enough information for evaluators to refer a child to a specialist for further testing, if necessary. The earlier that problems are diagnosed, the better opportunity of fixing or managing a problem. In the case of young Jorge, the school's screeners decide he is, in fact, ready for kindergarten.

Preparation for school starts at home, where parents teach life skills and some rudimentary academic information such as numbers and colors. Jorge's parents read him stories from the earliest ages and taught him songs and numbers, but did not engage him in enough physical activity to develop his coordination, something he will have to learn in school. Numerous studies show that children do their most intensive and important learning before the age of 6. Benjamin Bloom, in his 1964 book *Stability and Change in Human Characteristics*, showed that people learn far more in the first five years of life than during any comparable time period. These young children are impressionable, vulnerable, and open to new experiences in a way that will never happen again. And the information children learn at an early age stays with them forever. Although traumatic experiences may stay locked in a person's unconscious memory, early experiences lay the groundwork for future success or failure.

Many children are enrolled in preschool programs. In general, these programs help children. Early childhood programs have been shown to increase children's IQs, and children in preschool programs stay in school longer, are less likely to be designated for special education programs, and are less likely to cause behavioral problems.

There is no clear academic advantage of preschooling, though, partly because preschools tend to focus on socializing children and partly because there is substantially less research on preschools than on higher grades. But preschoolers are capable of more academic learning than many people realize.

By the time Jorge arrived at kindergarten, he knew numbers and letters, and was ready to learn more sophisticated concepts. Research shows that the fundamentals of math, science, language, and social studies, even basic problem solving, are within the grasp of most of these youngsters. It is time to expect more from preschool.

TECHNIQUES FOR TEACHING

Although instruction must be adapted to the special needs of preschoolers, fundamental teaching techniques proven to work for everyone also apply to children at this age: individualized instruction as needed, clearly defined expectations, and effective evaluation and correction.

The first step is determining the maturity level of the preschoolers, as this will determine expectations. The children must be able to accept simple instructions and be able to perform according to those instructions. The children need to have adequate attention spans and also sufficient independence from their parents to relate to the teachers. They also must have the physical coordination to complete simple tasks in sequence.

While older children can be assigned work based on previous test results, children under the age of 6 all start out with little available data on which to base academic decisions. Since the child's physical and mental maturity are the only guideposts for teachers to judge a child's readiness at this age, when in doubt the child should be started at the lowest level of academic knowledge and moved up according to performance. If students are able to perform the tasks they are assigned, they are assigned more advanced tasks. If their performance is inadequate, the students should be corrected until they master the task and then are able to move on to the next one.

Preschoolers require more attention than older children, and therefore teachers should have as few students as possible. Research shows that one-on-one tutoring is the most effective way to teach preschoolers, and student/teacher ratio should be no more than 5 to 1, although the total class size may be larger. While older children need to understand the details of their assignments and the criteria by which they will be judged, preschoolers can often find such information overwhelming. Instead, they only need to know the task itself. It is up to the teacher to show the student how to perform the task correctly and to judge the child's success as the child works on the task. Rather than test the youngster after the task is performed, preschool teachers should correct the student while attempting the task whenever possible.

The amount of time that a student spends on a task increases the chances that the student will master the task, but a preschooler's skittish attention span can be a limitation. These children are easily distracted by the activities around them and by their personal needs. In addition, it's easier to stay focused on games and fun than on academic exercises. But there are techniques that can help children stay on task for academic material, such as presenting the information in a play-like setting, and in small graded increments.

Repetition is a tried-and-true method of teaching, although some kinds of repetition are more useful than others. Teachers should use repetition in presenting information that is about to be taught; they should incorporate repetition into the lesson itself; and they should expect students to be able to repeat what they have learned. With younger students, the repetition must occur within a tight time frame, whereas older children can practice their new material later in the class or during their homework. For instance, a teacher can show how a letter is pronounced several times and then ask the students to repeat the letter. Repetition should not be used excessively, however. Students are being taught to think, not to respond like robots or animals. They should be taught procedures and behaviors in addition to rote information, and they should be taught how to conceptualize something before learning it, to begin training their intellect. For instance, Jorge's preschool teacher was offering a lesson in simple addition. Along with asking the students to repeat the information aloud—"one plus one equals two"—she shows them how one plus one equals two with different examples, such as apples and a student's shoes.

It is also important to begin to teach youngsters about the relationships between objects or events. Young students can begin to learn about the causes and effects of their own actions, as well as concepts such as simple maps or body parts. They can also learn about space relations, such as how rooms fit into a house; time relations, such as earlier/later and telling time; and social relations, such as family members and school officials.

Preschool teachers must have strong communication skills, since their little charges have limited language skills and a low tolerance for ambiguity. Teachers must make a special effort to speak distinctly, to use simple words, and to be specific, concrete, and relevant. They must be able to clearly define their expectations, and they also must be able to engage the students in helpful question-and-answer sessions.

One effective method to teach preschoolers is by allowing them to use concrete objects for their learning. The more senses that are involved, the better. For example, students learning about peaches should be allowed to see, taste, feel, and smell the peach, and hear the sound it makes when someone bites into one. Learning tends to proceed from the specific to the general, from the concrete to the abstract. Using concrete objects and all the senses builds a foundation for future learning of abstract concepts.

LESSONS FROM RESEARCH

Although competent research on academic learning among preschoolers is in short supply, a few good studies illustrate how these youngsters learn. One of the most interesting studies was published in *The Reading Teacher* in 1977 by D. W. Carnine, who compared two methods of teaching children vocabulary words.

In one group children were taught using a method called Phonics, in which the child was required to master the sound of one letter before moving on to the next. After the child mastered eight letters, she was presented with a word containing the letters learned. The teacher would show the child how to sound out the word and the child would then learn to sound out the word also, at first slowly and then at a normal rate. Another group of children were taught using the Look-Say method, in which whole words were presented to the child and the teacher would help the child say the word. In both cases, the children were taught individually and tested on the individual letter sounds, words that were similar to the learned words, and new words. The children who learned using the Phonics instruction tested significantly better than the children who used the Look-Say method. This study provides an excellent example of how preschool children use specific, concrete building blocks of language to understand larger concepts.

Math also can be taught at the preschool level, according to a 1996 study by H. Hong in the *Early Childhood Research Quarterly*. In this case, preschoolers learned math through storybooks such as "Goldilocks and the Three Bears," "Ten Brave Brothers," "A Wolf and Seven Little Goats," and "Good Brothers." The children were assigned follow-up activities, such as acting out the story or applying the story's math concepts to their own lives. They could also practice the math concepts during free play time with math materials. In some math categories—classification, number combinations, and shapes—the students performed significantly better than their peers, although they didn't perform better on a math achievement test. Nonetheless, this study shows that young children are quite capable of learning mathematical concepts.

Preschoolers are also capable of simple problem solving, according to a 1983 experiment recorded by A. U. Rickel and R. B. Fields in *Psychology in the Schools*. A group of children were read a story three times about a ball that was stuck under a bridge and blocking traffic, and were allowed to discuss the story. Two groups of children—one group that had heard the story and another that hadn't—were asked to find the proper way to remove an inflated beach ball from a birdcage. More students who had heard the story about the bridge released air from the ball than the students who hadn't heard the story.

Two other experiments confirm that children can learn academic concepts. A 1997 study by N. Toyama, Y. M. Lee, and T. Muto in the *Early Childhood Research Quarterly* showed that preschoolers who helped care for animals were able to learn elementary biology concepts, showing that science can also be learned at an early age. P. Wolff, in a 1972 article in the *Journal of Experimental Child Psychology*, reported testing children on whether playing with a toy helped youngsters remember it later. One set of children was given a pair of toys to play with, and the other set was asked to simply imagine playing with the toys. Those children who actually touched the toys were much better able to remember the toys.

Much more research is needed to understand how young children learn and to design the best strategies for them. But for now, the biggest barrier to teaching preschoolers academic subjects seems to be the small amount of time set aside for academic work. The children themselves are able to learn the material and teaching preschoolers rudimentary math, language, and science gives them a head start for elementary school and beyond.

STUDENT READINESS

Preparing students to learn—to take the next step in their educational journey—is a key objective of education at every grade level. Teachers can plan lessons in great detail, but if their students are not ready to learn the material or perform the task, the teacher and the students will fail. A person can't learn to drive a car or cook a meal without certain required skills and knowledge. Such is the case with academic learning as well.

Every academic goal must be achieved through a logical sequence of tasks, so that completing each task builds a stairway of success. The harder the objective, the higher the number of tasks needed to reach the top of the staircase. Teachers must evaluate whether students' knowledge, skills, and personal dispositions enable them to climb the stairs. Before aiming for a new goal, teachers need to evaluate students' previous performance and whether the students are ready to undertake the new task. Only when they are sure that the students have completely mastered the old material should new material be introduced. Young students need to have their learning solidified through repetition: the review of concepts and practicing skills.

If a student is mentally and physically ready to learn, if a teacher has prepared lessons that include an academic component, there is every reason to expect that preschoolers can learn basic math, science, and language skills. Indeed, failing to teach this material is a missed opportunity to lay the groundwork for future success. Jorge, for example, has been well prepared for school by his parents and his preschool teachers. He understands what is required from a student, and he has had sufficient success in preschool to build his self-confidence. Unfortunately, too often, when well-prepared youngsters enter elementary school, they find themselves unable to maintain their academic momentum, held back by the need for their less-prepared peers to catch up to them. The next step is to change instruction in elementary and higher grades to ensure a continuum of learning.

So much more can be done to take full advantage of the potential of preschooling when young people are so vulnerable and impressionable. Early learning is voluminous, potent, and indelible. It provides a foundation for later learning. Do we provide young people with a foundation that will crumble, handicapping them for the rest of their life, or do we provide them with a solid foundation that gives them a real head start in life?

More youngsters need to be preschooled. Parents who are capable of teaching their children the basics do not have enough spare time to make a difference. Often both parents work, and some parents hold more than one job. And the many illiterate and undereducated parents in America are incapable and need help. Although families have a greater influence on children than school, more than one-third of our youngsters are not prepared by their parents to succeed in school. They need preschooling.

Present-day preschools are successful in socializing young people. They teach children self-help skills, coordination, self-control, and social rules; to follow instruction; and how to relate to adults and peers—all of which makes it easier for children to adapt to school life. Fewer children who attend preschool drop out later on, fewer need special education, and fewer become juvenile delinquents. Still, preschool is far from reaching its potential.

Research shows that preschool does not significantly advance academic achievement, but it could. Preschoolers are perfectly capable of learning fundamentals of science, social studies, math, and language. Furthermore, methods of teaching academics to young people are well known. All that is needed is to include basic academic subjects in the preschool curriculum, especially reading and math, and to engage teachers qualified to teach preschoolers and the subjects.

Extending and enriching preschooling with basic academics is win-win for everyone—children, parents, education, and society.

HIGHLIGHTS

Nothing advances student achievement more than preschooling, especially when parents are unable to introduce their children to reading and math fundamentals. Before beginning formal education children should be given diagnostic readiness tests to pinpoint their inadequacies and make accurate placements. In addition to socializing children, preschools should teach basic academic and problem-solving skills. Research shows that preschooling ensures success in school, but instruction must be age appropriate.

3

Effective Instructional Strategies

Peter teaches a class of 24 fifth graders at a suburban elementary school. For today's math lesson he has prepared an instructional unit on fractions. First, he stands in front of the class and explains what fractions are and why they are important. He takes an orange and peels it to show the sections, and tells the class the fraction that each orange section represents. He takes out a roll of pennies and a dollar bill and shows how many pennies are needed to equal one dollar. Lastly, he slices an apple pie into unequal sections and shows the class the differences between the sections. While he makes these presentations, class members frequently interrupt with questions.

Then, Peter hands out a worksheet with some simple examples of fractions. As the class works on the sheet, he walks up and down the aisles. If he sees a correct answer on a sheet, he tells the student the answer is correct. If he sees an incorrect answer, he briefly discusses with the student why the answer is wrong and helps the student toward the correct answer. Nonetheless, it is impossible for him to correct every sheet on the spot, so he collects them to evaluate later. He then asks the students to develop their own questions about fractions for homework.

The next day Peter hands out the corrected worksheets and asks the students one by one to present their fraction questions. During these presentations Peter asks the students numerous questions and helps lead those who are struggling to the right answers. Of the 24 students, 10 clearly understand the concept of fractions at this point.

Peter breaks the class into three groups, spreading around the 10 students who understand fractions evenly and asks each group to develop a rudimentary household budget, given a specific income and certain expenses. "What percentage of the budget will be used for food? What percentage will be used for a mortgage?" he asks. As each group makes its presentation, Peter asks each member of the group questions. By the end of this day's lesson, 20 of the students now have a good understanding of fractions, leaving four students still struggling.

At this point, since the vast majority of students in the class have mastered the material, it's time for Peter to move on to the next instructional unit. But he asks the remaining four students to visit the school's tutoring center. He writes a report for the center's coordinator outlining the lesson he has been teaching, mistakes students made, and what instructional methods he had used. The students are given time through the rest of the week to attend the center and by the end of the week, they too have mastered fractions. The entire class passes the final exam on fractions.

The example is more complicated than it first appears. Peter is a sophisticated, well-trained teacher who has prepared his lesson well. He also has at his disposal a well-designed tutoring center. The technique here is called corrective instruction, in which a system of planning-instruction-evaluation-correction leads to mastery. Corrective instruction lies at the heart of effective education. Let's pull apart Peter's fractions lesson to understand how corrective instruction works. (More on tutoring will be discussed in Chapter 5.)

There are some underlying assumptions to corrective instruction. One is that almost all children can learn if they are properly taught. Another is that group instruction by itself is insufficient for many. There is ample proof of that, since a third of young people leave the education system either semiliterate or without a diploma.

To succeed, instruction must function as an effective system. A good example of how to build a successful system comes from the world of sports: the San Francisco 49ers football team. When Bill Walsh became the coach of the 49ers in 1979, he installed a system called the West Coast offense. That offense uses short passing routes to confuse defenses and control the ball. It also depends on every player performing an exact role and a script for play-calling. Walsh won three Super Bowls and the team won two more right after he retired, and several of his disciples have won more championships. The most striking feature of the West Coast offense is that it succeeds almost regardless of the individual players or the opponent. The players must have a minimum level of talent and must be willing to work hard, but turnover among the players doesn't affect the success of the system. The same process applies to teaching. Using effective instruction, almost any teacher should be able to succeed in almost any classroom.

The major components of the effective instruction cycle are planning, instruction, evaluation, and correction. Each of these components is essential and interrelated. Teachers must have the time and resources to adequately plan their lessons because without a solid, well-planned foundation, the rest of the system crumbles.

PLANNING

How did Peter prepare for his lesson on fractions? The lesson's genesis was in a policy objective set by the local school board or other policymaker. Policy objectives are broadly worded, designed both for public consumption and to guide the work of education professionals. In our example, the policy objective was "students will learn fractions."

These abstract concepts must then be translated into concrete learning objectives so that student achievement can be observed, evaluated, and demonstrated. A teacher must be able to observe students' progress toward a learning objective to help them. Ensuring that students meet the larger policy objective requires policymakers and professional educators to work together to create a useful road map. The learning objective is more specific than the policy statement. For example, "students will be able to add simple fractions," "students will be able to divide compound fractions," or "students will be able to solve word problems that require the use of fractions."

The next step on the road to the fractions lesson is to plan the instructional strategy for achieving that objective. The strategy is laid out as a sequence of instructional tasks. Instructional tasks are the essential building blocks of education. Like the strands of DNA that create all living matter, mastering task after task builds a helix of learning. Teachers plan tasks in a logical sequence, leading progressively from minimal, entry-level tasks to those that prove mastery of a learning objective. A student may learn the concept of halves, then thirds, then quarters, and so on.

If students fail to perform an instructional task, teachers clarify their misconceptions and turn to corrective tasks, which the students perform until they master the learning objective. If the original lesson was presented as a worksheet, for instance, the teacher may offer a struggling student something on a web site or an interactive video to vary how the material is presented. If the student masters the material at this point, the next step in the progression resumes.

A logical sequence of tasks to achieve a learning objective creates an instructional unit. While a certain amount of complexity may be required when organizing instructional units to meet a larger policy objective, excessive complexity within instructional units can overwhelm students, and even teachers, and impair learning. Students must be able to understand the teacher's expectations and the goals they are trying to achieve.

Although teachers don't have full responsibility for specifying the learning objectives, they are responsible for planning tasks to achieve those objectives, evaluating how well students perform those tasks, and reteaching the tasks to help students master them.

Once the teacher has planned the task sequences, it is time to get down to the actual job of teaching. The first step is for teachers to tell the students about the tasks they are to perform, how they are going to perform them, and why the tasks are important. Then the teacher has to help the students perform the tasks, evaluate their performance, and prescribe subsequent tasks based on that performance. Students who master the tasks advance while others receive corrective instruction.

The following instructional strategies have been tested in the classroom and by researchers. The effectiveness of these strategies in increasing student achievement is supported by research, ranging from 50 studies to more than 200 for each strategy. (Details can be found in Chapter 9.) Teachers can get better results if they incorporate these strategies into their teaching.

DEFINING EXPECTATIONS

The teacher's very first step when beginning an instructional unit is to define the learning objective, how the objective will be met, and how students' success will be judged. When students don't know the goal they are to achieve, what tasks they will be expected to perform, and how goal achievement will be judged, they can become confused or frustrated, and the learning objective will move farther away rather than closer.

The teacher must use simple, clear language to define the objective. In giving the students an overview of how they will achieve the objective, the teacher must clarify the sequence of tasks they are to master. Finally, in listing the criteria the students must meet to achieve an objective, the teacher must be very specific and do everything possible to avoid ambiguity. Failing to outline specific criteria may lead students to misunderstand whether they have mastered a topic.

These are techniques that can be applied outside the classroom, in everyday life. A parent may want her son to clean his room. That is her objective. The parent then lays out the procedure to achieve the objective: "You need to vacuum your floor, put your toys away, and make your bed." Specific criteria are then explained so that the child will know the parent will be satisfied when the carpet isn't dirty, the toys are in their proper place, and the bed is made.

Teachers use the same approach. To teach a youngster to identify the main ideas in a text, students might be asked to outline the topics in a sample of prose. The criteria for success might be whether the students can identify 80 percent of the main ideas in the sample. Another objective, from social studies, might be for students to identify each of the 50 states on a map. Students might be asked to memorize a map, and then correctly label 80 percent of the states on a blank map. For Peter's fractions lessons, the criteria for success may be getting three-quarters of the questions right on a test.

The keys to successfully defining expectations are clarity, specificity, and completeness. Teachers must first understand the goals and tactics for achieving them in an instructional unit, and then they must communicate those goals and tactics to their students. Students have to know where they are going, how they are going to get there, and when they have arrived.

PROVIDING CONTIGUITY

Contiguity is a teaching strategy that condenses time and space so students can immediately see how events are connected. When providing contiguity, teachers keep related events close together so that students learn how they are related to each other. An instructional unit is broken into small pieces and taught in a logical progression and as close together as time will allow. The teacher's feedback should also occur as quickly as possible, and corrective assignments should be given promptly, so that students maintain their focus on the lesson at hand. Contiguity is also important when disciplining a student; the punishment must take place soon after the infraction for the punishment to make sense.

In the classroom, contiguity can be shown through such examples as time-lapse photography of a bulb becoming a flower. A world map shows the relationships between countries. In language arts, contiguity among the parts of a short story is imperative to understanding the story as a whole. First and second graders see that letters of words must be printed contiguously for the words to make sense. For Peter's lessons in fractions, the teaching of fractions, the assessment of learning, and the corrective instruction all occur in quick succession.

Students can also apply the principle of contiguity outside the classroom. They will quickly learn, for instance, that studying for an exam right before the test helps keep information fresh. They will learn in sports or the arts that practicing a procedure step by step in quick succession helps to associate the steps together.

PROVIDING UNIFIERS

Students also learn more quickly and more completely when they are shown how parts are related to a whole; for example, how the different ingredients in a recipe are blended to make a cake. Teaching only an end result without teaching how smaller parts contribute to it, or teaching the smaller parts without also teaching the end result, are both insufficient. Teachers should use topic outlines, diagrams, hierarchical trees, tables of contents, flow charts, calendars, budgets, graphs, and other helpful tools to show how parts make up a whole. Older students can be taught to create their own unifiers; for example, their own course outline or vacation itinerary.

It's helpful to think of a jigsaw puzzle when trying to understand contiguity and unifiers. The pieces of a puzzle are kept together, not scattered about. Those working on the puzzle use the picture on the box for clues, and then they complete the puzzle piece by piece.

UTILIZING REPETITION

Another successful teaching technique is repetition. For Peter's lesson on fractions, students could be given several different worksheets to practice adding and subtracting fractions. This kind of learning is a product of repetition, which is easily misused but remains an important tool in the teacher's kit.

Often, teachers will teach new material and then save the repetition format for later homework, when repetition could have been easily incorporated into the original lesson plan to reinforce the message. For example, a teacher illustrating how to use a microscope might hand out material beforehand that described the correct procedure, show a sequence of pictures outlining the correct procedure, and then model the correct procedure herself. This process allows the students to conceptualize the procedure first before attempting it and reiterates the lesson in different ways. Afterward, the student would be given guidance in repeating his procedure in order to perfect his technique. Finally, students can be quizzed on the procedure and their mistakes corrected to solidify their learning.

Repeatedly testing students helps them to learn the material. However, it's important to vary repetition so that it doesn't become boring. Teachers can use different media to present information and can ask students to repeat information in writing, orally, through video, or through artwork.

A teacher might, for instance, teach an instructional unit on one day, assign additional work, and quiz the students. The next day he might review the information from the previous day, present new information, then quiz the students on both days' material. Youngsters use repetition in learning the alphabet, parts of the body, or the names of the states. It aids recall and perfects the performance of learning skills.

One method of repetition is *repeated exposure*. For instance, a student could look up the same word in different dictionaries. This provides some variety while still maintaining the student's focus on the one word. Another method is simply *practice*. A student can design her own math word problems so that she uses different wording to practice the same concepts.

Once students learn that practice can improve their skills, they can learn to use repetition themselves to perfect their performance. When studying on their own, students should learn to vary their tasks and keep their study sessions relatively short so the work doesn't become tedious.

Teachers shouldn't use repetition blindly, without explanation, as though children were pets to be trained. Once students understand the point of the procedure, they can begin practicing its execution and continue until they work smoothly with little or no error. Conceptualizing the procedure before beginning it allows students to monitor and correct their own behavior, much as golfers conceptualize the perfect swing.

CLARIFYING COMMUNICATION

How a teacher speaks is as important as what he says. Good communication is as much a conscious technique as repetition and contiguity. In teaching, as well as business and other endeavors, clear, simple language is essential. Imagine a military in which commanders spoke in vague terms and constantly digressed into discussions of their private lives. The troops would never get out of their barracks.

Teachers should avoid a halting flow of speech, eliminating such distractions as "er," "um," and "y'know." The topics should always be relevant to the subject matter. Their speech should be detailed and include concrete examples of the concepts being taught. Transitional words, such as "tomorrow we will" or "our next subject is . . ." should keep students' minds moving forward.

Teachers should tell students everything they need to know. This sounds simple but requires forethought. Teaches should explain the "why" of a concept as well as the "how," and should show the relevance of a concept to students' lives. Using the question-and-answer format is a well-tested and successful method. It sharpens students' understanding and clarifies concepts they may not understand. Students should be encouraged to ask questions almost any time.

Students also have an obligation to communicate clearly, and they should consciously be taught how to speak and write clearly. Students who communicate well in writing and speech are more likely to get higher grades. A student doesn't need to be naturally gifted to succeed in class, only well taught.

The rules of grammar and usage are important and receive far too little attention, but they alone do not comprise good communication. The key criterion is whether a student can effectively communicate an idea to others. Students must learn how to illustrate their ideas, how to communicate precisely, plainly, and without digression. In their presentations they must learn to show cause and effect, and relevancy. Their presentations should be in different forms—such as video or with photographs—and engage different senses.

These are skills that can and should be taught. Here's one exercise: A student describes a picture of a building to his class. The class is given four pictures of four different buildings and must choose the one he described. The more students who choose the correct building, the higher the grade. Afterward, the class discusses what the student might have done to elevate his score.

Teaching young people to communicate succinctly in writing and speech is an essential element of good education, and these skills can't be taken for granted. They must be taught and practiced.

USING REMINDERS

The next time you stick a Post-It note on your refrigerator to remind you to pick up your dry cleaning, think about how reminders are used in the classroom. In education, there is a continuous need for students to recall factual information. One effective method is teaching reminders—little clues to retrieve the information from memory. Even note taking in the classroom is a form of reminder.

Those memory joggers can take many creative forms, such as acronyms, rhymes, catchy phrases or tunes, numerical or alphabetical sequences, or rules (e.g., "I before E except after C"; "Every Good Boy Does Fine"; "HOMES"). For many thousands of students, these little reminders bring back memories of grammar, musical notes, and the names of the Great Lakes, respectively. Scientific formulas and math symbols such as + are a form of reminder. These mental Post-It notes are especially useful for information that may not be directly relevant to a student's life.

In addition to being taught some of these time-tested reminders, students need to learn how to create their own mental Post-It notes. Useful reminders include to-do lists, outlines, and creating their own rhymes or songs to remember information. The students in Peter's fifth grade class could be given a homework assignment to create their own reminders about halves and quarters, for instance, and present them to the class.

TEAMWORK

Research shows that the most effective teaching is one-on-one, but teaching teamwork promotes peer tutoring, which is also an effective way to teach. Teaching teamwork to young people is, in and of itself, a worthy goal, since teamwork will be essential to their future work and social lives. Groups of students can be utilized for special projects, to learn educational games, and to help enforce rules of conduct. After-school activities such as sports and debating rely on teamwork as well.

Research also shows that the optimal size of a team workgroup is four or five. In creating teams, teachers should analyze whether individual students are ready to succeed in the team format. Before the specific assignment is given, the small groups should be given team-building exercises to let them get to know each other and build rapport. They might, for example, interview each other about their background and common interests. Teachers should stress the importance of cooperating to attain group goals and rewards during this early process.

Teachers should present the team goal and overall strategy to be learned to the entire group, and the individual team members should receive specific instruction about their own roles. At this point, the team begins working together on the assigned task. Brainstorming solutions and mutual assistance should be encouraged. Students should get whatever help they need whenever they need it.

Evaluations should be conducted of both individual and team performance, with appropriate corrective teaching. Teams should be recognized for their degree of progress, but individual students should be held accountable and should not be allowed to hide behind the team.

When Peter broke his class into three groups to learn fractions by building a rudimentary household budget, he was effectively using the teamwork technique. Whether teamwork is used to present a class play, construct a science project, role-play a math problem, or practice soccer, the skills young people learn will make them better students and citizens. The peer tutoring that results from teaching teamwork also improves the learning and performance of team members.

TRANSFER OF LEARNING

This skill is important because all of the learning accumulated and stored in memory over the years is worthless unless it can be transferred and applied to solve problems in the present. Transfer of learning tends to be automatic in dealing with simple tasks in the present, such as recalling the name of a friend you meet in the street. On the other hand, transfer of learning to perform more complex tasks, such as balancing a checkbook or assembling a bicycle, often requires a deliberate, conscious thought process.

Deliberate transfer requires teaching students how to select a procedure to perform a task based on having performed similar tasks in the past. The more similar a task is to a task the student has performed previously, the more likely that the student will succeed. It's important that students choose procedures they are able to perform, rather than choosing procedures at which they can or will fail.

As they teach their lessons, teachers should highlight for students how certain procedures can be applied to future problems. Students should learn how to select a procedure that is identical or similar to other procedures previously used to solve problems. When a student selects a procedure to solve a problem, he should be expected to explain and defend his choice, using appropriate analogies. Then he should test the effectiveness of his choice and evaluate the results.

Several other successful techniques for ensuring student success—keeping students on task, providing ample teaching time, and providing ample learning time—are discussed in Chapter 6. Providing decision-making instruction is discussed in Chapter 7. The following section illuminates the essence of effective instruction: how to teach the majority of students who don't master material on the first try.

The science of teaching, like the science of medicine, requires rigorously tested methods, consistent application, and accurate diagnosis. A surgeon can't walk into an appendectomy operation and wing it; there are protocols for an appendectomy that she must follow to achieve the desired outcome. Surgeons plan out an operation, and each step of the operation must be part of a logical progression. Every member of the surgical team knows his task and understands the goal. This same approach holds true in school, a place where the success rate must also approach 100 percent.

USING CORRECTIVE INSTRUCTION

Teaching is easy when students master information on the first try. Not many teachers, or students, can claim such an easy life. The greater challenge is correcting students, or reteaching them material until they master it completely. "C's" and "D's" may be passing grades, but they indicate far less than mastery and often signal serious learning deficits that impair future learning. Failure to master material leads to a steady rate of dropouts as students fall farther and farther behind. Reteaching material in different ways until a student has mastered it has been shown by research to be enormously effective, yet schools consistently fail to provide all of the corrective instruction students need to succeed. Peter knows, for instance, that four students in his class are having trouble mastering fractions. Should he simply abandon them?

Corrective teaching, like everything else in the classroom, requires good planning. Teachers should understand how to fix a problem before the problem gets worse. For each instructional unit, the teacher needs a main lesson plan as well as several corrective tasks. Corrective tasks must be short to allow for frequent evaluation, and as simple as possible. Students who do not master the material on the first try must be assured that they will receive all the help they need and that concerted effort on their part will result in success. (This assumes that the students are ready to learn the material.)

There are two ways to correct a student: *spontaneous correction* during teaching and *remediation of inadequate test performance*, which includes reteaching material, homework assignments, and student projects.

Spontaneous correction happens in the classroom as the students are learning new material. During oral question-and-answer teaching, correct answers should be acknowledged as correct. For incorrect answers, teachers can provide and explain the correct answer if they think the mistake was simply careless. If a teacher thinks students do not comprehend the correct answer, the teacher can prompt and hint toward the correct answer or reteach the material. While monitoring work students are doing at their desks, teachers should acknowledge and discuss correct performance, point out and discuss incorrect performance, and show students how to correct their mistakes.

For correcting inadequate test performance, it is vital that teachers prepare corrective tasks before teaching the material for the first time to ensure student progress toward the learning objective. Students who test inadequately should be assured that they will receive all the help they need and that their concerted efforts will bring success. Teachers should discuss the test performance with students, show the students how to correct their mistakes, offer corrective exercises, and then retest the students. This cycle is repeated until mastery of the material is achieved.

This process is similar to teaching a child to hit a baseball. The coach models the proper stance, shows the proper swing, and tells the child to "keep your eye on the ball." The child steps up to the plate and takes a hopeful swing at a pitch. If the child misses, the coach evaluates the child's performance, tells her what she did wrong, shows how it should have been done, and then lets the child take another swing. This is repeated until the child gets her first memorable hit.

The same technique works in the classroom. Someone teaching basic algebra might ask a series of questions designed to evaluate how well students understand the equations. If a student answers correctly, she recognizes the achievement, but if a student answers incorrectly, she may patiently ask him the same question in different ways, leading him to the correct answer. If several students have trouble with the correct answers, the teacher may reteach the material. The teacher may then assign a series of algebra problems for students to practice in class. The teacher circulates among the students, commenting and acknowledging correct answers and correcting wrong answers.

Let's say the lesson is about nineteenth-century U.S. history. The teacher may teach a unit about the Industrial Revolution and the migration of farm workers into cities. She may ask the students a series of questions about how and why factories were created, and the formation of labor unions. The students would answer questions about the history lesson, and the teacher would identify which students are having trouble learning the material. She may offer a new set of questions to a few students while other students who have mastered the material read an essay about foreign immigration. Once all the students seem to have mastered the material in this unit, she may ask them to construct an outline of the Industrial Revolution as homework.

In an English class, students might be asked to learn the difference between a noun and a verb. In class they might be asked to construct a list of as many verbs and nouns as they can. Students who clearly don't understand the difference between a noun and a verb would be given additional instruction and then retested. For homework, students might be asked to observe activities around them and to record them in terms of nouns and verbs, such as Dad (noun) starts (verb) the fire (noun) in the grill (noun); the dog (noun) laps (verb) his water (noun); the bicycle (noun) has (verb) a flat tire (noun); and so on.

Corrective instruction, with adequate instructional time and one-on-one teaching, makes the difference between students who learn everything they need to know and students who learn only random bits and pieces. Note that effective corrective instruction can only be done one-on-one. While material can be taught at first to the whole class, and some projects may involve groups of students, students must receive their critiques privately, away from their classmates, and each student should get his own course of corrective action. After all, classes don't get graded, individuals do. All students make mistakes. Most can tolerate their mistakes if they feel they have a fair chance of learning the material. Students who have hope of succeeding will also learn the valuable lesson that persistence pays off.

Teachers who are burdened with nonacademic busywork or students who are dragged to assembly after assembly lose their focus and instructional continuity. Too often the students who get the most attention are not the ones who need the attention, and only the efforts of interested parents may draw the teacher to someone like Beth, a quiet youngster who might not be grasping all the material. A well-planned system of assessment and corrective action ensures that virtually all students learn all the material.

Ensuring student success requires adequate quality and quantity of teaching. Schools need to provide more time for teaching, and the standards for teaching need to ensure teaching proficiency. Better teaching can be achieved by using techniques and strategies that have been proven to work, such as those described above. More time for teaching must translate into more time per pupil, so that these youngsters master their assigned tasks and reach their learning objectives.

EVALUATING PERFORMANCE

How can a teacher tell whether the performance of a task meets the criteria for success? Through evaluation. There are three parts of the evaluation process that need to be considered.

- Criteria must be established to define correct performance of a task and when a learning objective is achieved.

- Testing must be done to assess actual performance. Testing may be as simple as a teacher observing and describing a student's performance or as complex as constructing an extended test to assess whether a student has mastered a number of tasks.

- A procedure must be used to compare actual performance with the criteria for correct performance. Comparisons may be as simple as comparing one student's spelling of a word to the correct spelling of the word, or as complex as comparing students' test scores to predetermined criterion scores to indicate whether criteria have been met.

Testing is essential to describing and evaluating student performance. To be useful, tests must be *valid, reliable,* and *objective.* To be valid, a test must assess the performance of tasks that were assigned. The content of the test items has to correspond to the content being taught. To be reliable, the test must yield consistent results when given repeatedly to the same or similar students. If the scores aren't consistent, the test items are modified. To be objective, the test must show consistent results when scored by different people.

Two types of tests promote objectivity: *scoring key tests* and *scoring criteria tests.* In a scoring key test, the correct or best response is designated for all test questions. Scorers do not need to judge the correctness of the answers. In fact, scoring key tests can be machine scored. Examples include multiple-choice tests and true-false tests. In scoring criteria tests, scorers do need to judge the students' responses and statements. Criteria are provided to the person judging the test, and the scorers compare the responses to the criteria. Scoring criteria are used to evaluate term papers, essays, student projects, and oral exams. Scorers are trained to apply the criteria until they become proficient in using them.

Let's say students are learning the periodic table for chemistry. A scoring key achievement test might ask students to match the name of the element with its symbol, either as a simple list or through multiple-choice questions. In the same chemistry class, the teacher might use the scoring criteria approach to judge whether a student can explain a lab project by writing a report.

Here's an example from social studies: A teacher might develop a multiple-choice test to evaluate how well students have learned important dates from the Revolutionary War, or students might be asked to write an essay about a major event that happened during the same war. In the language arts, a teacher might evaluate the vocabulary of students through a multiple-choice test or through a book report. The usual standard for mastery in both kinds of tests is 80 percent.

Timing is important for effective evaluation. Teachers can't wait until report cards are issued to diagnose students' weaknesses. Evaluation must take place early and often, as close to the performance as possible while the task is still fresh in students' and teachers' minds. When it comes to marking a test, there are only two marks students need after they have performed a task: "Mastery" or "Not yet." This moves away from the stigma of failure and fairly reflects student progress.

Report cards also need to spell out specifically where the students have performed adequately and where they have not. An "A" on a report card could signify that a student has 10 percent or fewer inadequacies in a subject; a "B" could signify that a student has scored between 11 percent and 20 percent inadequacies; a "C" 21 to 30 percent; and so on. The report card should outline a student's own path in achieving learning objectives rather than to compare her with the rest of the class, which is a pointless exercise. In addition, students need and deserve an explanation of their inadequacies, not just a grade.

Before students are promoted they are required in many states to pass a comprehensive achievement test to certify that they achieved grade-level objectives. Students who were given all the corrective instruction and evaluation they needed should have little difficulty passing these achievement certification tests.

INSTRUCTION IN FOCUS

A report card is not the end of the learning process but part of a continuous loop of learning. The system proposed here of planning, teaching, and evaluation is based on decades of research, and the techniques suggested here are field-tested and proven. Planning involves laying out sequences of tasks to achieve the learning objectives, for both initial and corrective instruction, and determining procedures for evaluating achievement of those objectives. Teaching entails facilitating student performance of task sequences, task by task, until the objectives are achieved. Evaluating involves comparing student task performance to criteria for mastery. Students who master the criteria move on to the next sequence while students who haven't mastered the material receive corrective instruction until they do.

The focus of this system is instruction, because research has proven that all but the most psychologically impaired students can achieve all learning objectives through high school. The difference between one student and another is the amount of effective instruction needed to achieve the objectives. School facilities, counseling, equipment, busing, and other factors may be essential to keeping school in session, but instruction has the greatest and most direct impact on learning. How teachers are taught is a key element to successfully implementing instruction. For both trainees and veteran teachers, good research needs to be brought into the classroom.

Since research shows that teaching techniques rather than teacher traits are responsible for increasing student achievement, the focus of pre-service and in-service teacher preparation should be on perfecting teaching strategies, many of which were described in this chapter. Effective teachers are not born—they are developed through education. Likewise, the emphasis should be on teaching evaluation rather than teacher evaluation. Teachers with strange characteristics can be very effective at teaching. Besides, most personal traits may not be alterable through teacher education. Applicants for teaching positions can be screened for traits that preclude proficient teaching, such as garbled speech.

Despite all the evidence that a successful school system is attainable, far too many students fail to achieve learning objectives through high school, objectives that most of them are capable of achieving. If the medical system had such a high rate of failure, it would be a scandal, but society would never permit it. The failure rate in education can be substantially reduced by using proven instructional techniques, providing ample corrective instruction, and basing instruction on frequent diagnostic evaluation.

HIGHLIGHTS

Teacher preparation should begin with an orientation to the instructional process: (1) planning, (2) teaching, and (3) evaluation. Within this context, pre-service and in-service teacher education should focus on perfecting instructional strategies proven to increase student achievement. Those strategies are introduced in this chapter and in Chapter 6, and are summarized in Chapter 9. Teacher preparation should no longer neglect the teaching of evaluation skills. Teachers must be taught how to construct accurate achievement tests and to aggregate test scores to assign grades. They need to be able to confidently defend their tests, test results, and grades to students, parents, and grievance committees, and in courts of law.

4

Instructional Programs

Jorge, the young kindergarten student from Chapter 2, may enter school and find his teachers working with programs called Learning for Mastery or Direct Instruction, formal educational systems that are supported by research.

Interested citizens need to know how to tell the more effective programs from the less effective ones. It's worth noting that many of the successful programs contain effective instructional strategies described in the last chapter and in Chapter 6. These programs feature good planning, corrective instruction, evaluation, immediate feedback, and other techniques that are effective in teaching any subject.

LEARNING FOR MASTERY

One program that might sound familiar is called Learning for Mastery, a well-researched program that improves student achievement by 64 to 93 percent. It is based on the work of John B. Carroll, a professor at the University of North Carolina, who demonstrated that almost all students can achieve all learning objectives required through high school. The difference between students is only the amount of instructional time each student needs to succeed.

Learning for Mastery contains the following elements:

1. The teacher judges the students' readiness to undertake the subject to be taught. For instance, do the students know enough about the parts of a sentence to learn about prepositions?

2. The material is divided into units, with each unit building toward the next one.

3. The teacher determines what material students must master in order to move on to the next unit. The teacher also designs alternative ways to teach the material to students who don't learn it the first time.

4. The teacher outlines to the class the procedures to be used, what students are expected to learn, and how they will know they have mastered the material.

5. The students begin their tasks as soon after the teacher's instructions as possible.

6. The students are tested as soon after completing the unit as possible.

7. The teacher provides immediate feedback on the students' test errors. The teacher assigns the corrective alternatives.

8. Students who need more instruction are given it.

9. Teachers spend most of their time on instruction and as little time as possible on administrative functions.

In this program, students are afforded the time, instruction, and other assistance necessary to master a learning objective; the system works for students from kindergarten to college and beyond. Learning for Mastery has been well researched and is a solid, effective program. For more information about Learning for Mastery, you can read J. H. Block and L. W. Anderson's *Mastery Learning in Classroom Instruction* (New York: Macmillan, 1975).

DIRECT INSTRUCTION

Direct Instruction is another program that research says is effective. Highly structured, it emphasizes teacher-directed instruction and supervised classroom assignments. Skills are taught step by step, building on previously learned skills. As with Learning for Mastery, Direct Instruction can work for students in all grades. This program can be used for math, English, science, history, and reading. Instruction, practice, and evaluation are built into each lesson.

Direct Instruction contains the following elements:

1. Teachers begin each lesson with a review of the previous unit.
2. Teachers offer a short statement on goals and objectives.
3. Teachers demonstrate the tasks students are to perform to achieve the objectives, giving explicit, step-by-step instructions.
4. Students perform the tasks immediately following instruction.
5. Teachers prepare a large number of questions and, during instruction and student practice, ask these questions to check how well the students are learning the lesson. This is called guided practice.
6. Feedback and corrective instruction are supplied immediately after students are evaluated. Teachers should confirm correct answers and encourage students who are still working their way toward understanding the material.
7. If a student makes a careless error, the teacher should give her the right answer. If a student gives an incorrect answer and the teacher thinks she doesn't know the material, the teacher can either give the student hints toward the correct response or reteach the material.
8. Before assigning work to be done at a student's desk, the teacher must make sure the student is able to work on the material without assistance. Work that is to be done at a student's desk should be assigned right after the guided practice session, and should be directly relevant to what is being taught.

Direct Instruction relies on the question-and-answer technique to prompt and assess learning, and also on a tightly constructed, orderly process of teaching, practice, and evaluation. Research shows that this program increases student achievement. For more about Direct Instruction, see M. C. Wittrock, ed., *Handbook of Research on Teaching* (New York: Macmillan, 1986), especially the report by B. Rosenshine and R. Stevens on teaching functions.

SUCCESS FOR ALL

A major component of Success for All, known by the name Roots and Wings, is for elementary students and focuses on language arts, math, social studies, and science.

Success for All is based on the belief that students require a meaningful context to learn to read, and they also need skills to attack word and math problems. These skills help build students' ability to solve problems. Success for All also emphasizes teamwork.

The program called Reading Roots is for youngsters in kindergarten. It employs the following tactics:

1. Letters and letter sounds are introduced to the students orally, and then students move on to written symbols.

2. Students are then taught to build letter sounds into words, sentences, and stories.

3. Students learn about story structure, comprehension, self-assessment, and self-correction.

4. Instruction also includes cooperative group reading and story activities.

5. Students receive one-on-one tutoring as necessary.

Reading Wings is for students in grades 1 through 6. In this program, students learn about story structure, prediction, summarizing, vocabulary, and story writing. Teachers focus on reading comprehension skills, which students practice in teams. Students are grouped by reading level for practice and tutoring, and cooperative activities help students learn together.

There is considerable research on the effectiveness of the Success for All language arts program. In one study, conducted in 1996, researchers used 12 techniques from the Success for All program over six years, including tutoring, cooperative learning, and a focus on comprehension skills, and those students showed significantly higher achievement than similar students in other schools.

A program called Math Wings is also designed for students in grades 1 through 6. It balances problem-solving skills with teaching children about abstract concepts. Games, computers, and other tools are used. Students work in cooperative groups to discover and apply math concepts, and student performance is frequently assessed.

Although there is more research on the Success for All reading program, the research for Math Wings is adequate enough to show its effectiveness. For instance, one 1989 study showed that first graders using this cooperative learning program performed significantly better on complex addition and subtraction word problems than students in first grade classes that didn't use the program. The study focused on teacher training. First grade teachers were given training on research, how children solve problems, how to use problem solving as the focus of instruction, how students can apply what they already know to what they are learning, and how to continually assess student performance. In another study, in 1984, the emphasis was on grouping students of different abilities, while also allowing students to work at their own pace. Students in the cooperative learning classrooms performed significantly better than other students, possibly because of peer tutoring.

There is not as much research on the Success for All social studies and science program, however. The program is called World Lab, and its goal is to integrate social studies and science with reading, writing, math, and fine arts. Students do role-playing; work in small, cooperative groups to investigate topics; and use fine arts, music, computers, video, and other technology to prepare multimedia reports.

Success for All offers a teacher tutoring component aimed at first and second graders. (Other tutoring programs will be discussed in the next chapter.) The focus of the Success for All tutoring programs remains on context and word-attack skills. Students also build their vocabularies to help identify words that are hard to decode.

There are four components to the Success for All tutoring program. First, children learn to read by using texts that are meaningful for them. Second, phonics—learning to sound out words—needs to be taught to help children decipher words. Children read stories that are relevant and interesting and yet have a phonetically controlled vocabulary. Third, the students need to be taught to link words with comprehension. And finally, students are taught strategies for becoming better readers. Students receive tutoring 20 minutes a day for as long as they need it, and the tutor works closely with the classroom teacher to make certain the lessons are in sync with what is being taught to the rest of the class. Students are assessed every eight weeks.

A typical tutoring session begins with the student reading a familiar story aloud. This is followed by a one-minute drill in which the student practices letter sounds learned in class. The rest of the session involves the tutor and the students reading stories together. In these shared stories, the narrative is interesting and predictable, with important vocabulary in large type and the other elements of the study in small type. The student reads the vocabulary words and the teacher reads the smaller type. The tutor asks questions about the story and has the student read passages aloud. There is some writing as well.

The tutors are certified teachers who also teach reading classes. The tutors and the regular classroom teacher use a form that includes an assessment of the student's problem and which lesson is being taught in the classroom to ensure that the tutoring relates directly to class work. Tutors receive six days of training on the Success for All program and on tutoring in general, and are given weekly feedback by supervisors who observe their work. Tutors are trained to teach students to question themselves. For instance, after reading a chapter, a student would be expected to ask herself, "Did I understand what I just read?"

The Success for All program's focus is on problem-solving skills and understanding. The goal of education is not merely teaching the alphabet or the multiplication tables, but to produce young people who can digest and analyze and put to use the never-ending stream of information that will wash over them in their lifetimes.

For more information about this program, call the Success for All Foundation at 1-800-548-4998 or write to the foundation at 200 W. Towsontown Blvd., Baltimore, MD 21286.

ACCELERATED SCHOOLS

There are several other well-known programs that have little research support. One of those is the Accelerated Schools program, which addresses at-risk children in all grades. The goal is to move them through the curriculum quickly. This program appears to have serious flaws. Most importantly, it does not allow adequate time for students to correct their performance.

Accelerated Schools uses these tactics:

1. Teachers lay out the material to be learned and then students teach each other in peer tutoring sessions.

2. Concepts are taught in ways that relate directly to students' lives.

3. Students are asked to discover for themselves how to apply the concepts they are being taught.

4. Substantial attention is given to the arts and physical activity.

5. Outside assignments and homework are mandatory.

The pace of instruction is fast, to keep students engaged and focused, and teachers spend almost all of their time teaching. But there is no time set aside for evaluating and correcting individual student performance.

TEACHING THE TEACHERS

Problems in the classroom are not always the fault of a teacher, but sometimes the fault of the way the teacher was trained. Too often, teachers are not proficient in the programs they are using or are using techniques that are unproven. Before entering the classroom, teachers should be observed and corrected in the program they will be using until they become proficient. There is another problem when teachers are not taught well—it becomes difficult, if not impossible, to evaluate the effectiveness of a program if the teacher is not certified or competent to administer it.

Three teacher training programs that have been reviewed lacked well-defined curricula or supporting research: the New Mexico Collaborative for Excellence in Teacher Preparation, Discovery (based in Ohio), and the Mathematics and Science Teacher Education Program in San Francisco. The New Mexico program joins new teachers with more experienced mentors. Discovery links colleges with public schools for professional development. The California program created a network of schools to provide training for new teachers. All three programs, while well intended, seemed to lack definition and supporting evidence.

When deciding how to improve instruction in your school system, it's important to consider the advantages of both instructional programs and strategies. Learning for Mastery, Direct Instruction, and Success for All have their own distinctive formats. Each has been proven effective by research and each incorporates some but not all instructional strategies that have been proven effective. Teachers trained to be proficient in using them can be expected to be successful. Teachers are, however, required to teach according to the rigorous format imposed by the adopted program. Many teachers balk when their discretion and ingenuity are restricted. They like to be free to provide corrective instruction and enrichment as they see fit.

The alternative is to teach teachers to be proficient in applying the 15 effective instructional strategies summarized in Chapter 9 and described earlier. They would be well prepared for success and have more latitude to be creative and to adapt to classroom demands.

HIGHLIGHTS

A number of instructional programs are available. Research supports the effectiveness of some of these programs in increasing student achievement but not others. Learning for Mastery and Direct Instruction are examples of programs that are effective in teaching most subjects. Others are effective in teaching specific subjects, such as reading and math, which are taught in most remedial programs. Some programs lack definition and are difficult to replicate. Private companies offer programs for students who fail in public school and whose parents can afford the price. Successful programs utilize many of the instructional strategies described in this book.

5

The Power of Tutoring

Joe is a ninth grader who is doing poorly in science class. His parents are hardworking and well-meaning, but neither was able to attend college. They don't have enough time to help Joe with his homework at night, nor do they have the money to sign him up for private classes. Joe's teacher knows that the youngster is falling behind and assigns him extra homework, but the extra homework leaves him even more frustrated. Joe gets a "D" in science.

In the same class, Kelly is also struggling. But her parents both went to college and are able to help her with her homework. Her parents also make more money than Joe's, and they hire a tutor for her after school. Kelly manages to get a "B" in the science course.

Kelly is not necessarily smarter than Joe; she is simply more fortunate. Parents' education level and income often determine their children's future, making America the Land of the Lucky rather than the Land of Opportunity for far too many youngsters. One answer to Joe's problem is quite simple, however: one-on-one tutoring.

Imagine an educational system twice as effective as the current system. Imagine children receiving enough instruction so that almost all of them could succeed in school. Imagine that this system does not need to increase the cost of education very much, and would save society an enormous amount of money in the long run. That's what preventive tutoring can do.

Students who receive tutoring are dramatically more likely to achieve academic success than students who only learn in classrooms. About 90 percent of tutored students attain a level of academic achievement reached by only 20 percent of students taught in conventional classrooms. The average tutored student outperforms 98 percent of students taught in the conventional setting. One-on-one tutoring to supplement classroom instruction reduces special education costs, dropout rates, and illiteracy. It can reduce the number of people who are institutionalized because they can't take care of themselves or are a menace to society.

Preventive tutoring shouldn't be confused with remedial tutoring. Remedial tutoring is for students who are failing already (and will be discussed next). Remedial tutoring usually takes place instead of regular classroom instruction, in a different room with a different teacher. Preventive tutoring is designed to keep failure from happening and takes place in conjunction with classroom learning. Preventive tutoring is based on a diagnosis of a student's misconceptions, and requires coordination between classwork and tutoring. Preventive tutoring is not simply supplemental, or extra, work; it is an essential element of academic success.

PREVENTIVE TUTORING

The principle of preventive tutoring relies on three assumptions:

- That students will be given as much instruction as they need to keep up with their class;
- That tutoring will be planned according to the needs of individual students; and
- That classroom teachers do not have enough time to give all students all the personal instruction they need.

Individual instruction during class is woefully inadequate, despite teachers' best intentions. Teachers get distracted by other students; most classwork is designed for group instruction; and class sizes are rarely small enough to allow teachers to spend enough time with each student.

The focus of preventive tutoring is on teaching the topic the student is having difficulty with in new ways. Teachers provide preventive tutoring to correct students' mistakes as time permits. The need is so great that other tutors must be found, including peer tutors, volunteers from the community, telephone tutors, or a tutoring center. Preventive tutors do not need to be certified teachers, although some guidance should be provided before they tutor and as needed while they are tutoring. It is essential that tutors thoroughly understand the topic they are teaching. They also must be made aware of the mistakes they are to correct and have a copy of the class textbooks and workbooks used to teach the topic. Tutoring should be available for all subjects and for all students at all grade levels, although the earlier needy students get tutoring, the better. Preventive tutoring doesn't have to be expensive or elaborate; it just has to exist.

Parental tutoring is inexpensive, convenient, and very effective. Just helping their child with homework can go a long way toward preventing failure. There is no stigma attached to being helped by a parent. Parents can offer a variety of enrichment opportunities to stimulate their child's interest, such as magazine subscriptions and visits to museums. Parents can identify misconceptions in the tests and assignments their child brings home, and they have access to the teacher for clarification and advice. Involving parents directly in the instruction of their children is enormously productive for student, teacher, and family. Schools can provide short workshops for parents to help them develop their preventive tutoring skills. It could reduce the school's failure rate.

But many parents, like Joe's, are simply unable to help in a sustained way. Schools can establish a network of tutors, whether paid or volunteer, who are available to students by telephone. This type of program is cost-effective. The calls are private, and the tutors should be available and convenient. The biggest drawback is the absence of face-to-face involvement that can engage a student's enthusiasm and help a tutor evaluate whether real learning is taking place. But telephone tutoring is certainly better than no tutoring at all.

Students also can get help from their peers and online. Peer tutoring can be successful and cost-effective, depending on how the program is designed. Peer tutors are best used for specific, well-defined, short-term tasks. These students may not require extensive training, but they do need orientation and guidance on tutoring before they begin and as needed while tutoring. They also need to know the mistakes they are to correct and have available the class textbook covering the topic the student needs help with. Under no circumstances should a peer tutor be assigned to a student with pronounced learning disabilities. Although older students often tutor younger ones, same-age tutoring can also work well. In fact, one reason that heterogeneous groupings work better than ability grouping is that more advanced students pitch in to help their peers.

Many tutors are now offering their services over the Internet. One problem with this relatively new phenomenon is that it can be hard to check a tutor's qualifications. They may not be competent or able to accurately diagnose the root cause of a problem. The best tutoring is one-on-one and face-to-face, where the tutor can monitor nonverbal communication and watch the students perform their assignments. Through personal observation, a tutor can prompt and direct desired performance, correct mistakes, and provide encouragement as the students go along. Computers can serve as an aid to tutors and be used to supplement assignments, but they are no substitute for live preventive tutoring.

Another form of tutoring, albeit a hotly debated one, is home schooling. Home schooling has its faults, but it also has some virtues that are relevant to this discussion. Children taught in the home get individual attention. Parents who undertake home schooling need strong backgrounds in basic subjects, and parent-teachers can receive support from home-schooling publications and networks, including access to specialists who can teach sophisticated subjects. Home-schooled children who have won national spelling and geography contests highlight the benefits that tutoring provides.

REMEDIAL TUTORING

Remedial tutoring should be provided when preventive tutoring is insufficient to prevent a child from failing. Remedial tutoring is done by teachers who are certified in special education and have been trained to teach students who are unable to succeed in regular classrooms. They learn teaching techniques that work with children who have various learning difficulties. They have a special orientation and commitment: "If a child can't learn the way he is being taught, then teach the child the way he can learn." An Individual Education Plan is designed for the child based on diagnostic data, and the child is taught accordingly. Typically special education teachers are assigned to teach children with learning difficulties specified by disability laws, such as mental retardation. They are also better prepared to teach children without such learning difficulties who are unable to succeed in the regular classroom. Here are some of the programs and remedial techniques they use.

Some remedial tutoring programs are designed to teach language basics to students with specific sensory deficits, such as dyslexia. Some programs are designed for all ages; some are just for the youngest learners. Some focus on language skills; others include math. A few better-known programs are listed here to give you a guide for judging a school's programs.

Reading Recovery. Reading Recovery is one of the best-known tutoring programs. The program, developed by Marie Clay in 1985 in New Zealand, steers clear of the phonics/whole language controversy. Rather, it emphasizes the development of phonics skills as well as the use of contextual information to assist reading. The program is intended to be a short-term, one-on-one tutoring program for first graders. The Reading Recovery program is administered in half-hour blocks for 12 to 16 weeks. During these sessions, children read many small books. Some of the books are written in a way that simulates speaking, while others use a language that children can readily anticipate. They also read slightly more difficult texts than they have tried before. Children compose and read their own stories, and use magnetic letters. Each tutor must be a certified teacher and receive a year of training. The tutors attend weekly seminars where they are trained to observe, diagnose, and assess youngsters, and to develop individualized programs. During their training, tutors participate in weekly "behind the glass" demonstrations where they observe, critique, and discuss tutoring sessions with their trainers. Follow-up training continues after the first year. As the tutors work with the children, they keep a detailed record analyzing student performance. Reading Recovery is a registered trademark of Ohio State University.

TEACH. TEACH was developed in 1990 to diagnose reading problems and address specific deficits. The program covers first and second graders and focuses on four areas: prereading, such as the ability to recognize and organize symbols; word-attack skills, which use phonics to decode words and identifying whole words; comprehension, which requires a rich vocabulary and the ability to draw inferences; and study skills. The program focuses on matching, copying, recognizing, and recalling letters and words more than on other reading skills. Students receive 30 minutes of tutoring three to five times a week. Tutors are certified teachers. For more information, contact the Prevention of Disabilities Program, Learning Disorders Unit, New York University Medical School.

The Language-Experience Approach. The Language-Experience Approach is a technique to be used when conventional reading programs have failed, leading students to feel frustration. The program addresses first, second, and third graders. The tutor asks students to tell stories about happy personal experiences, and together they write stories in the students' own words. The students read the stories aloud after each new paragraph is written. Although there are no specific requirements for the tutors, they should have enough experience teaching reading to provide remedial assistance to the youngsters. For more information, contact Marvin Efron, 1212 Canary Drive, West Columbia, SC 29169, 803-794-3444.

There are several other tutoring programs that are highly structured and come with their own materials. These are essentially tutors in a box and can be very effective.

The Orton-Gillingham Instructional Program. The Orton-Gillingham Instructional Program uses action-oriented, multisensory training to teach reading and spelling. Reading and spelling are taught at the same time, and students also learn the history of language and grammar. The learning is structured, sequential, and cumulative, and students review old material until they have mastered it. Teachers must take 45 hours of course work and 100 hours of supervised practice. For more information about this program, contact the Language Tutoring Center, 3229 Debbie Drive, Hendersonville, NC 28739, or call Educators' Publishing Service at 1-800-225-5750.

The Wilson Reading System. The Wilson Reading System was first published in 1988 and focuses on training teachers. The carefully sequenced, 12-step program helps students decode words and allows students to proceed in small increments. Like the Orton-Gillingham program, students use all their senses in the Wilson Reading System. Tutors are trained for two weeks and use material supplied by Wilson, including manuals, rules notebooks, test forms, sound cards, and word cards. For more information, contact Wilson Language Training, 175 West Main Street, Millbury, MA 01527-1441, or call 508-865-5699.

The Lindamood-Bell Clinical Instruction Program. The Lindamood-Bell Clinical Instruction Program is based on the Socratic question-and answer technique, in which students learn to correct themselves and become independent thinkers. The program teaches reading, spelling, and math. The tutor is called a clinician and is expected to follow the program precisely. There are two types of tutoring: regular, which is one hour a day for four to six months, and intensive, which is four hours a day for four to six weeks. For more information, call 1-800-233-1819.

The Laubach Literacy Program. The Laubach Literacy Program is aimed at teenagers and adults, and focuses on helping people address everyday literacy problems. The program consists of four levels that correlate approximately to the first through fourth grades, and culminates in a diploma. Tutors require no special training but are expected to use the materials supplied by the program. For more information, contact Laubach Literacy, 1320 Jamesville Avenue, Box 131, Syracuse, NY 13210.

Interestingly, the free market has stepped in where many schools have failed by making a profit on tutoring. Private tutoring companies offer after-school programs for people who can afford them, such as the Kaplan

Learning Centers, Kumon Math and Reading Center, and Sylvan Learning Centers. Kaplan Inc. is owned by the Washington Post Company and is a national provider of education services for individuals, schools, and businesses. At a Kaplan subsidiary called Score, students build academic and goal-setting skills in what the company calls a motivating, sports-oriented environment. Kaplan, which serves all ages, and Score, which goes through the eighth grade, rely heavily on computers. A Kumon Math and Reading center also doesn't use textbooks. Rather, students work on a sequence of timed worksheets and are then tested on the material. Students correct all of their mistakes before moving on to the next worksheet. Sylvan Learning Center offers services that are closer to the classroom model. Teachers sit in the middle of a horseshoe-shaped table and teach small groups of students. They usually have time for one-on-one tutoring as needed. Each student receives an assessment test, and an individual program is created to address his or her academic weaknesses. Positive reinforcement is emphasized. Students must master concepts before moving on to the next task, and students are retested periodically on material to ensure they have truly learned. These private centers can be effective but expensive, and many families cannot afford them.

All of these tutoring programs are unique and have different strengths and weaknesses. But they have one thing in common—they offer students a chance to learn material they are unable to learn in the regular classroom. Reading and math are the foundation of education; all future learning contains elements of one or both of these skills. Clearly, there are a variety of techniques and programs that can be offered to help youngsters with reading and math, but whatever the choice of approaches, a tutoring program must be offered. It is inexcusable to allow Joe to fail and Kelly to succeed simply because of an accident of birth.

Doctors don't prescribe one treatment for all their patients; schools can't teach students without providing instruction that accommodates personal differences among students. In education one size does not fit all. Each student comes to the classroom with different skills, interests, and talents. Furthermore, students require different amounts of instruction to achieve the same learning objectives. Group lectures where new material is introduced are only the starting point for learning. The teacher must then begin to assess which students have learned the material and which have not, and to assign work that is appropriate for each student. Students who continue to struggle can't be abandoned. Both student and teacher need the added support of a well-designed, adequately financed, one-on-one tutoring program. Such a program is not a luxury; it's as necessary to a school as desks and ball fields.

CORRECT DIAGNOSIS

Successful intervention depends on accurate diagnosis. The best solution becomes obvious when a problem is pinpointed through testing. A doctor may think she understands a patient's problem after listening to his complaint. She can be much more certain of the correct diagnosis and treatment after she runs tests.

Three types of diagnoses are used to remedy deficits in students' learning: preventive diagnosis, remedial diagnosis, and clinical diagnosis.

Preventive diagnosis is made by a classroom teacher who identifies mistakes students have made on class assignments and tests. The purpose of this diagnosis is to prevent academic failure. No additional testing is required. The mistakes disclose the problem and preventive tutoring is arranged to correct the mistakes and misconceptions that underlie the mistakes. Preventive tutors need nothing more than knowledge of the mistakes and the student's workbooks and texts used to teach the topic the student is having difficulty learning. A tutor who knows the topic and how to question students to assess learning works with the student until he masters it. The tutor may be a teacher, a peer, or a volunteer from the community, perhaps a retiree or a person employed locally. Preventive tutoring should not be expensive, nor should it make a teacher's job harder. It is designed to offer the supplemental tutoring needed by students in every class because teachers simply do not have time in class to offer all the preventive tutoring needed.

Remedial diagnosis is used to diagnose the *academic* problems of students who have failed to learn. They have not kept up with their classmates and need special education to succeed. Tests designed to pinpoint academic problems are used, including diagnostic reading and math tests, because these tests reveal deficits that prevent the learning of other subjects. A special education teacher continues to provide remedial tutoring until test results indicate that students are able to succeed in a regular classroom or need to be placed in a special education environment to continue making progress.

Clinical diagnosis is done to identify underlying causes of failure to learn. Teachers make referrals to school psychologists, nurses, or administrators, as school policy dictates, when they suspect that a student's learning difficulties may be due to a physical or mental disorder. A teacher may suspect a student has a vision problem when she detects him squinting with his face close to a book he is straining to read. When Horace kept asking his teacher to repeat what she said, the teacher suspected that his learning difficulty may be due to a hearing problem and referred him for diagnosis.

Educators diagnose academic deficits. Clinicians diagnose physical and mental problems such as poor vision, poor hearing, slow development, poor physical coordination, or hyperactivity. Students given a clinical diagnosis are treated by a clinician, often the person who diagnosed the problem. It's risky for teachers to try to treat a clinical disorder. When a student is failing class assignments despite the teacher's efforts to help, the teacher should refer the student for diagnosis. The teacher passes on all the records she has on the student, including notes on her observations.

Schools need to have systematic diagnostic procedures, and the faculty should be aware of them. Teachers must be responsible for preventive diagnosis as a part of their daily routine. Preventive diagnosis is the basis for prescribing instruction. Teachers must also be responsible for making student referrals when their efforts to help failing students are insufficient. Schools, nurses, and psychologists should receive referrals. They are trained to determine the diagnostic procedures appropriate for students; school administrators are not. The person receiving the referral decides whether remedial diagnosis, clinical diagnosis, or both are indicated by the student's records. The student should be seen personally if more information is needed.

DESIGNING A MASTERY CENTER

An effective tutoring program is provided through a special center, with its own location, director, and resources. These centers, which could be called mastery centers, need not be terribly expensive, but they can play a critical role in ensuring student success.

Let's return to the freshman science class, where Joe sits in the fourth row, quietly falling behind his classmates. One day he walks by the new mastery center and, after hesitating briefly, he walks in and tells the center's director that he's having trouble with science. The director makes an appointment with a tutor, and sends a note to the classroom teacher to make sure that the teacher knows that the student is seeking assistance.

This kind of mastery center provides diagnostic and tutoring services not only for children who have failed in the classroom, but also for students who might be in danger of failing. It can therefore be a tool to prevent failure. If students are allowed to use the tutoring program without requiring a referral from a teacher, more students are likely to seek help when they need it, not when someone else notices they have a problem. If students are allowed to refer themselves, they may prevent their own failure. The ability for self-referral also reduces the stigma of tutoring. Just as important, the tutoring is aimed at achieving mastery. Students who are performing marginally at a "C" level can elevate their grade to "B" or "A."

Typically, though, the referral process begins when a teacher notices that a student is having trouble with an assigned task, by a written test or through direct observation of a student's performance. In Kelly's case, the teacher stayed after school a few days to help her with the work, and also assigned her to do a special project, but Kelly still struggled. At that point, the teacher made a referral to the mastery center. The teacher included a written explanation of why the referral was being made and documentation of the student's difficulty. The purpose of the referral is further diagnosis of the student's clinical and academic needs. The teacher writes a report for the mastery center's director, outlining observed difficulties, and forwards it along with the student's records and failed tests and assignments.

The location and design of the mastery center itself is important. It must be a quiet place without distractions. The center should be open before, during, and after school. Some tutoring programs are offered in community facilities such as houses of worship and community centers, and even in students' homes. Ideally, the center would have an open-door policy and be available for students to simply drop in without an appointment, although appointments should be available as well. The stigma that may be attached to students who require special services may be reduced or eliminated if the tutoring center is used by the whole student community. To make the center more attractive, advice and enrichment can be provided for any student on request. Many students who are succeeding in class want to learn more. Curiosity and desire for self-improvement are terrible things to waste.

Although tutors themselves may be part-time, the mastery center should have a director, a full-time professional who majored in special education. The director finds and trains tutors, diagnoses academic inadequacies that require corrective instruction, ensures that students with physical or mental problems receive clinical diagnosis and treatment, coordinates tutoring with classroom instruction, monitors tutors' progress, and provides good facilities for tutoring. The director also stays abreast of new research and new programs. If a tutoring program is essential to a good school, the mastery center must be managed by a director who is expert in academic diagnosis and corrective instruction.

The center also must have a variety of alternative teaching methods and materials available so that the proper program can be provided to all types of students, and simple screening tools, such as eye charts, for deciding whether to refer a student to a specialist. The center itself may not necessarily require a lot of extra teaching materials and resources, as long as those resources are available from the teacher, the school library, or some other source.

Good tutors can be found practically everywhere. Some possibilities include teachers, retirees, parents, other students, civil servants, and business employees. Some corporations encourage their employees to tutor school children part-time.

A school could start slowly, one grade at a time, and expand the program. Once the commitment is made to a mastery center, the financial commitment won't be far behind. Young people who leave school illiterate and incompetent are ill prepared for the job market or family and civic responsibility. Many become drug addicts, criminals, and wards of the state. Diagnosis-based instruction and mastery centers would more than pay for themselves in the long run by increasing student competence and reducing failure and dropout rates.

HIGHLIGHTS

The average tutored student outperforms 98 percent of students taught in conventional classrooms. Classroom teachers do not have sufficient time to provide all their students with all the tutoring they may need to succeed. Preventive tutoring on topics students are struggling with prevents failure and can be administered by part-time volunteers and peers. Remedial tutoring of disabled students is administered by special education teachers. Programs are specially designed to teach students failing in school. Successful teaching depends on the accurate diagnosis of student deficiencies. Performance on class tests and assignments is sufficient for prescribing preventive tutoring. Remedial tutoring is often based on results of diagnostic tests designed to reveal underlying causes of failure to learn.

6

Time Management

Time is as much a part of the classroom as textbooks and chalkboards. If time is inefficiently or inappropriately managed, a student can be set as far behind as if her textbook were written in Greek. Time is a commodity, a tool, a resource. Used wisely and consciously, time can make the difference between academic success and failure for many students.

Time management falls into three categories: the school year, the school day, and an individual class. Increasingly, experts are arguing for more time in the school year—for tutoring, for extracurricular activities, and for adequate teaching time on academic subjects. The typical school year format is based on a farming schedule that has long since become irrelevant while, at the same time, educational expectations have been rising. In addition to addressing increasingly strenuous academic requirements, extending the school year and the school day may reduce juvenile delinquency and the amount of time youngsters must fend for themselves. Extending the year would also give curriculum planners more flexibility and opportunity for focusing on academic subjects.

In the classroom, teachers must spend their maximum effort and time on academic subjects and minimize the amount of time they spend on planning, busy work, or nonacademic subjects. The more time a teacher spends actually teaching, the better the students' chances of actually learning. Most importantly, every child needs to be given enough time to learn material thoroughly, and they must be told repeatedly that they will get that time. Children must feel confident that even if they don't master a unit on the first try, they will get as many chances as they need.

Here's an example of poor time management: Emily, a fifth grader, is assigned to read *Black Beauty*, the well-loved "autobiography" of an English horse. Emily and her classmates are given five days to read the book, but only the swiftest readers in the class actually finish the book on time—about eight children out of 18. Emily has a history of trouble with reading comprehension and although she gets about three-quarters of the way through the book, and enjoys the story, she must read slowly and often rereads paragraphs and sentences. On the fifth day, the teacher hands out a quiz about the book requiring three short essay answers. After the quiz is turned in, the teacher facilitates a short discussion with the class about the book, but with only 15 minutes allotted, cannot include every student in the discussion. Emily gets a "C" on the quiz, skating by without fully understanding the lessons of the book and without drawing any attention from the teacher. In this example, the teacher failed to provide enough time for everyone to read the book, failed to ascertain whether everyone had in fact read the book, and failed to leave enough time for a full discussion that would have disclosed how many children had not read the book to the end.

Teachers themselves are not alone in their failure to manage time effectively. Far too often, instructional planners and administrators do not put enough thought into how much time to allocate for the achievement of instructional objectives. They spend much of their efforts on the curriculum itself without considering how the curriculum will be taught. Planning, evaluation, and feedback are rarely included in an instructional unit. Furthermore, time is not allotted to compensate for teaching time interrupted for administrative tasks, assemblies, announcements, and phone calls, almost all of which set a class behind.

Another factor is students themselves, who are rarely taught how to manage their time effectively. Students typically rush through their work or do not allow sufficient time to understand thoroughly the topic they are studying. Teaching students good time management skills is nearly as important to their future success as an academic subject. Think of the number of college freshmen who find themselves ill prepared to juggle the many requirements of their new lives. The wasted time, money, and emotional energy of these young people could easily be reduced if they are taught how to manage their time from an early age. Fewer freshmen will be overwhelmed if they have mastered time management.

Parents can see the results of time management in their own homes. For instance, a father might be teaching his son how to mow the lawn. First, Dad must ascertain whether Junior has the physical skills, emotional stability, and mental acuity to properly maneuver the powerful machine. Next,

Dad demonstrates how to use the lawn mower himself while Junior pays close attention. Junior then gets his chance to use the lawn mower, carefully supervised by his father long enough for Dad to feel confident that the lawn mower will be properly handled. Finally, after adequate practice, Junior is allowed to mow the lawn himself. But the work of learning does not stop there. Once given the responsibility of mowing the lawn, Junior must spend enough time on the job to leave the grass neatly groomed.

In the same way, school administrators, teachers, students, and parents must work together to ensure adequate time for teaching and learning. Teachers need enough time in the classroom to teach material, evaluate students' progress, and reteach as necessary, and students need enough time to practice and master the material. The better prepared someone is to learn a task, the easier the task will be. No conscientious parent would leave a teenager alone with a lawn mower without adequate training; the same should be true for learning math.

PROVIDING AMPLE TEACHING TIME

More than 60 research studies show the benefits of increasing the amount of time that teachers spend teaching. Research also shows that students learn more effectively if they are guided, rather than if they attempt to learn on their own. Students who don't receive enough guidance learn haphazardly, if at all.

Most teachers are constrained in the amount of time they can teach, though. It is difficult, if not impossible, for teachers to accomplish their work if administrators add extra classroom chores, and very few teachers have sufficient after-class time for the special tutoring so many students need. It is essential, therefore, for much more classroom time to be devoted to teaching.

Teachers must make the most of the precious teaching time they have. Capturing and holding students' interest in the lesson at hand is essential. Humdrum repetition or speaking in a monotone bores students, causing them to mentally leave the scene. Entertaining students with fun and games may attract their attention, but it may divert them from the essence of the lesson. To keep students interested and focused on the learning objective, teachers must use their ingenuity to make instruction pertinent to the students' lives. Well-conceived examples and illustrations relevant to students' lives make lessons unforgettable.

Why do students tend to lose their appetite for school around fifth grade?

Because the curriculum has become less important to their daily lives. Prior to fifth grade, they are acquiring language and math skills that are obviously necessary to them, whereas in later years the relevance of more abstract learning is not immediately apparent. It is the teacher's job to show them that relevance. Done properly, such teaching does not need to use gimmicks or tricks, which consume precious time and distract from the learning objectives.

Classroom time is most efficient when used by teachers to guide students as a group. During classroom time, students usually should not be assigned independent activities, such as silent reading or writing assignments, that can be done at home. In the classroom, where the teacher has the students together as a group, the primary activity must be guiding and correcting student performance, reviewing previous material, and presenting new material.

The classroom is also not the place for planning. Teachers must be given time outside of class to properly prepare their lesson plans and daily activities. Classroom time shouldn't be spent getting organized for the day's lesson.

Whether to include nonacademic subjects, such as the arts, during classroom time is one of the most hotly debated questions surrounding public schools today, and reasonable people disagree on the value of these activities. Academics must come first. Music, painting, and other nonacademic subjects are valuable, to be sure, and their inclusion in the school week makes a good argument for extending the school year.

In planning their time, most teachers recognize that younger students need more attention and guidance than older students, and that complex tasks require more teaching time than simpler ones. Teachers also need to leave enough time in their day for question-and-answer sessions. Students need to be reassured that they are not expected to master material immediately, and they also need to know that they are expected to ask questions and require assistance.

KEEPING STUDENTS FOCUSED

Nearly 170 research studies show that children need adequate time to complete their assigned tasks in order to succeed. Students who might otherwise succeed can fail if sufficient time is not set aside for an assignment. One of the greatest teaching challenges is keeping students focused. Students bring to the classroom different levels of attention, energy, and commitment. The system proposed in this book, under which students receive personal and consistent attention, requires teachers to ensure that each child is mastering material and also argues that sufficient classroom time must be spent on academic subjects. Only proper time management can keep both students and teachers moving forward together.

There are several tactics teachers can use to properly manage classroom time. Assigned work should be directly related to a learning objective, so students can clearly see the reason they are expected to master a task. The work must be appropriate and achievable, and instructions must be detailed and clear. Teachers should use the question-and-answer technique to ensure that students understand their instructions before beginning work. If the work is too hard or beyond the students' understanding, students will be unable to meet expectations and may begin to fall behind. Similarly, if students aren't given enough time to master a task, they will fail or perform below their potential. Teachers should spend time demonstrating new material, guiding students, and answering questions.

If independent work is assigned, teachers must be confident that the students are ready to work alone and that the independent work is as well planned, relevant, and well organized as lectures, demonstrations, and discussions. Independent tasks should be assigned to immediately follow guided practice activities, to solidify the learning. Most important, independent classroom activity must be supervised. If students are left alone to learn material they haven't mastered, progress can't be measured, mistakes can't be corrected, and success can't be ensured. Too often, the urge to doodle or daydream will overpower students who are left unsupervised. Finally, teachers need to minimize disruptions and distractions. One of the most effective ways of maintaining attention is keeping information flowing in a tight, logical progression so that students can see how each new element is linked to the earlier one. Teachers must also enforce their previously announced consequences for student disruptions, which will be discussed in more detail in the next section.

In a science class, for instance, a teacher may explain to the entire class a certain lab experiment, how the experiment is conducted, and how its results relate to a larger learning objective and their life. She would then demonstrate the experiment herself. Students would be encouraged and expected to ask questions, and at the end of her demonstration, the teacher would discuss the experiment with the students to ascertain whether they understand the technique and the larger objective. The students would then perform the experiment themselves, with the teacher patrolling the room to answer questions and promote proper technique. All of these steps require adequate time for planning, explanation, questions, and execution. Rushing through even one of these steps endangers the students' prospects for successfully concluding the experiment and learning the material. Relevant homework should be assigned to solidify classroom learning.

In addition to setting aside enough time for instruction, teachers and administrators must set aside enough time for corrective teaching in case a student does not master a task on the first try. Furthermore, ample time must be planned for all assigned tasks, such as in-class learning, homework, library projects, and labs. (In virtually every classroom, there are one or two students who cannot master the material regardless of how much time the teacher spends with them in the classroom. At that point, a teacher may refer a student for further evaluation. (See Chapter 5 for more on corrective tutoring.)

The amount of time spent on a subject affects how well the subject is learned, yet instructional planners routinely fail to budget enough time for students, focusing their planning efforts instead on the instructional tasks themselves. In addition, the time spent on some tasks, such as multiplication tables, is easier to estimate than time spent on other, more complex tasks, such as conducting library research. Individual skill levels also influence how much time it may take to complete a task. Planning adequate time is therefore an art as much as a science that improves with experience.

If time were treated as a finite resource, like cash or water, teachers and administrators might pay more attention to its efficient use. Students cannot be forced to pay attention to material that is irrelevant, nor can they be forced to study when left without guidance. In both of these circumstances, students can't be blamed for staring out the window or goofing off. But a strategy of well-planned, guided classroom work made relevant to their lives, with adequate time for questions and corrective teaching, can keep students involved and interested.

THE STUDENTS' ROLE

Learning is a two-way street. Teachers can't force children to learn; students must be willing participants in the educational process. Just as teachers must make efficient use of time, students must also learn to manage their own time effectively. And just as teachers have tactics that can improve their time management, so too do students.

Students should plan and organize their study time, and allow a sufficient amount of time for the task before them. Effective study sessions can range from half an hour to two hours at a time, depending on the students' maturity. But more than one session can be planned in a day.

Young people need a place to study that is comfortable, quiet, and well lit, where they will be free from intrusion and interruption. Any resources that might be needed—books, equipment, Internet access—should be nearby so the students don't have to keep getting up and looking for whatever they need. Many students believe they can study effectively with MTV blaring or wearing a Walkman; this is probably wishful thinking.

Students also should be honest with themselves when they have not mastered material needed to perform a homework assignment. Attempting a homework assignment without the prerequisite knowledge will lead to frustration and diminished performance. Students can sometimes become too embarrassed to ask a question in class or may not always recognize the source of their difficulties. At such times they can relieve their anxiety and save time by preparing some questions to ask their teacher or parents privately. They should also be encouraged to volunteer for tutoring. Teachers should encourage students to be frank about their learning difficulties, letting them know that help is available and they are not expected to master tasks on the first try.

An interesting 1984 study shows the difference between students who are given ample time to learn material and students who may not yet have mastered time management techniques. One group of fourth and fifth graders was told to work on a spelling and reading task until it achieved 100 percent mastery. Another group was told that the goal was 100 percent accuracy, and it was allowed to determine the amount of time they needed to work on the task. The result: the first group scored 12.49 points higher in spelling and 12.80 points higher in reading than the second group.

Students should be explicitly taught time management techniques in school, just as they are taught sportsmanship and citizenship. Often, there is a youthful impulse to rush through schoolwork. Students should be taught how to estimate the time needed for a task or project, and why spending enough time on a task is important. Students should be expected to write several drafts of a report, for instance. They should learn to set aside enough time for repetition and review of material, and they should also be expected to spend enough time on a project to perfect it. Learning to estimate and allocate enough time for a task is a skill that will serve a youngster well throughout his or her lifetime. Students can be taught to record the completion time of their homework assignments to improve their ability to judge how much time they require to complete various types of assignments.

BEHAVIOR MANAGEMENT

Children who are disruptive affect their own learning and the education of the entire classroom. Disciplinary problems can drain a teacher's energy and waste enormous amounts of time if not handled properly. Teaching is hard enough without trying to teach in the midst of chaos. The difference between teachers who can successfully control a classroom and those who can't is how they introduce their classroom rules and then how consistently those rules are enforced. Students who infringe on their classmates by acting out, seeking attention, or otherwise disrupting class need to be dealt with swiftly and surely. Dozens of research studies point the way to effectively managing classroom disruptions through five tactics:

- Rules of conduct and consequences for violating them need to be spelled out during the very first meeting with students.
- There shouldn't be more than five rules, and they should be brief and clear, so that students can memorize them.
- Teachers should ascertain as quickly as possible that students understand the rules and consequences for violating them.
- Consequences must be meted out promptly and briefly after a violation, with as little disruption to instruction as possible.
- Disruptions can be minimized in the classroom through nonverbal prompts, such as eye contact, and verbal ones, such as saying, "Keep your hands to yourself."

These methods are tried and true, and consistent application of them should make classroom disruptions a negligible part of the school day. It's worth noting that there is no evidence that allowing students to participate in establishing rules of conduct reduces classroom disruptions. The key to managing classroom disruptions is clarity and consistency of enforcement on the part of teachers and administrators.

Responding to violent incidents is more complicated than simply maintaining order in a classroom, and there is less research on effective methods. While there are 150 studies on how to manage relatively minor classroom disruptions, there is only a handful relating to how to manage violence in school. One study, conducted in 1978 by the U.S. Department of Health, Education and Welfare, found that four qualities could promote school safety: fair, firm, and consistent rule enforcement; the quality of academic instruction; student involvement in decisions; and low student/ teacher ratio. While this study is an interesting start to understanding school violence, it hardly qualifies as a prescription for success, and subsequent research raises questions about some of its conclusions.

Dealing with school violence falls to administrators more than teachers, and those administrators have an arsenal of punishments, including in-school suspension, out-of-school suspension, and expulsion. Unfortunately, in-school suspensions don't address the causes of violent behavior. Students serving an in-school suspension may be tutored, counseled, or simply stuck in a classroom with a glorified babysitter. The tutoring may help a student catch up to his class, but none of the tactics can ensure that a violent student becomes nonviolent. Out-of-school suspensions have no demonstrated effect on improving student behavior whatsoever, and only enforce a student's feeling of rejection and alienation. High school dropouts are twice as likely to have been suspended as non-dropouts, and many students who are suspended are supported by their peers and see the punishment as a reward, especially teenagers. Removing students from school with an expulsion may be easier on administrators and on classmates, but kicking a child out of school certainly doesn't help that child. Transferring violent students to alternative schools also makes life easier for administrators but does not necessarily rehabilitate the student. Warehousing a violent student with other violent students is not a strategy that is designed to help the students.

A clue to successfully managing violent students might be found in a 1992 study showing that where school discipline practices were lax, students were more apt to feel threatened and to bring weapons to school. It is possible that the same philosophy many cities apply to street crime—addressing lower-level crimes to prevent larger ones—might help prevent unhappy students from becoming violent ones. In other words, a student caught vandalizing a bathroom should be treated seriously and referred for in-depth evaluation to prevent that young vandal from turning to more violent crimes. A nip-in-the-bud policy can work in school. But a zero-tolerance policy can backfire, leading to overburdened administrators and driving some students away from school prematurely.

At least 300 intervention programs are available for students with violent attitudes or behaviors. There is almost no scientific research available to support these programs, however, and even the little evidence that is available fails to endorse one program over another. One of the most popular is called Second Step: A Violence Prevention Curriculum. Its goal is to increase social skills and reduce impulsive and aggressive behavior. The program features fifteen 50-minute classes that cover information about violence and training in empathy, anger management, and interpersonal problem solving, using role-playing activities. In some studies of program effectiveness the program was administered by peers, in others by teachers. In all studies, classes that were administered the program were compared to classes that were not administered the program. In peer-led classrooms there was a significant improvement in attitudes about violence, but in none of the classrooms was there a decrease in violent behavior.

There is no magic answer to dealing with violent students, but there are ways to intervene before students are tossed out of the school system. It seems likely that firm, fair, and consistent rule enforcement as early as possible, excellent academic instruction made relevant to students' lives, and student involvement in their education may address problems before they rise to the level of violence. Teachers and administrators need to spend enough time on discipline to ensure an orderly learning environment.

Just as parents often like to know *what* is taught in a classroom, they should start asking *how* a subject is being taught. Do curriculum coordinators budget enough time for an instructional unit? Do teachers have adequate time to plan and teach their lessons? Are children given enough time to ask questions and complete their assignments? Is classroom time scheduled for academic subjects given over to other subjects or entertainment?

These questions are just as important as knowing a school's reputation because the answers will indicate whether children are given ample opportunity to learn the material they are being taught. A surgeon planning a quadruple heart bypass must make sure that every step of the surgery is well planned—preparation, operation, and postoperative recovery. He wouldn't rush through such an important procedure, because rushing will lead to mistakes. Similarly, students and teachers shouldn't be rushed through the instructional process. Some learning can take place in an instant—but most learning takes time.

HIGHLIGHTS

Time management by both teachers and students affects academic achievement. Student achievement increases when students spend more time focused on assigned learning tasks and are given sufficient time to complete assignments, and when teachers spend more class time teaching toward the achievement of instructional objectives. Classroom disruptions can be controlled if rules of conduct are specified at the first class meeting and enforced. Present methods of controlling school violence and crime, such as suspension, leave a lot to be desired.

7

Motivation to Learn

Imagine two seventh grade math classrooms side by side. In one, the students are lethargic. Some are staring out the window. The teacher writes an algebraic formula on the chalkboard and tries to explain it to the bored class. One girl checks her watch, willing the minute hand to move faster.

In the second classroom, the students are engaged in a lively discussion about whether one of the students can ever save enough money from his part-time job for a new DVD player. Perhaps he must increase his hours—that changes one part of the equation. Perhaps he could find a cheaper device—that changes another part of the equation. The students work on the problem in small groups while the teacher walks around the classroom giving hints and correcting mistakes.

The difference between the two classes is obvious. In the second one, the students are given a relevant, real-life problem to solve as an incentive to learn, while in the first class, the students are being force-fed a dry formula that bears no relationship to their lives.

This example goes to the heart of where education should be headed. The goal of education is not to stuff children's heads with dates and formulas, but to prepare them to be useful, productive citizens. Well-educated students are those who know how to think critically, how to solve problems, how to work well collaboratively, and how to innovate. But children must want to learn what they are being taught; they must be active partners with their teachers. Students control what they are willing to learn. In order to be successful, teachers must plan not only what they will teach but how they will teach it, and that plan must provide students with incentives to learn the material.

Children are born with a strong desire to learn. Their first lessons are ones in survival—eating, crawling, crying for help, and eventually walking. Children enter school with an avid curiosity. As soon as they are able to separate from their parents and concentrate on schoolwork, they become interested in what school offers them. They learn how to communicate and work with others; they begin to master various tools; they test new ideas. They learn in a physical, hands-on way. Almost everything they learn through the elementary grades helps them deal directly with the things and people around them. They are highly motivated to learn what is being taught because the lessons immediately improve their own lives and their ability to cope with life's challenges.

In the middle school years, however, schools begin teaching more abstract concepts. Students are less able to see how these concepts help them. They are required to do more memorization of material that is not as meaningful to them. Learning becomes less interesting, and students become less motivated. From this point on, a student's success depends largely on the values of her family. If the family places a high value on education, students will force themselves to push through the boredom and irrelevance of their lessons.

Why do schools fail to maintain students' interest? How can schools build a true educational partnership with students, a partnership that makes learning seem essential and fascinating? By finding a way to interest students in the lessons they teach. Students need no incentive to learn; they need incentives to become interested in many of the academic subjects they are taught.

To interest students in their lessons, teachers must tap into what motivates them, keeping in mind that students are often not interested in subjects that adults think are priorities. That motivating factor can't be specific to individual students, for lack of time and resources; it must be broad enough to apply across large groups of students most of the time. The motivating drive must also be socially appropriate and not have unwelcome side effects. Hunger, for example, is not an appropriate motivation force to try to satisfy in the classroom. Eating during classroom instruction interferes with teaching, as would other motivations such as revenge, sex, and greed. Furthermore, students shouldn't be bribed to learn their lessons, since the goal of learning would then become acquisition rather than the learning itself. Teachers need to appeal to a motivating force that is healthy for students, compatible with schooling, and common among students. There is no single motivating force that dominates and preoccupies people all the time. People are complex and often are torn between conflicting motives. Even addicts are conflicted.

The most effective motivational strategy is to appeal explicitly to young people's inherent desire to control their lives. Children are born helpless, with virtually no control over their environment. As they grow older, they spend much of the rest of their lives trying to extend control—over their jobs, their families, their homes, their hobbies, their friends, their bodies. In fact, most of us spend our waking hours trying to control something, whether it's buying a new car, getting a promotion, or losing weight. In the classroom, young people respond to teachers who are willing to share the responsibility for learning, who can harness children's inherent desire to control themselves and their environment. And teachers can design lessons that enhance students' perception of their ability to control behaviors and outcomes. In other words, learning to control processes and outcomes is more than a means to an end; it's an end in itself. And as students are taught to influence their surroundings and behaviors, they are also taught their other lessons along the way. This motive—the control motive—is an essential tool for teachers trying to engage students in a learning partnership.

Lecturers are ineffective when they describe facts without relating the facts to students' lives. Nothing conveys relevance more impressively than showing students how they can apply the facts to improve their control. In college, describing an application may be sufficient. College students, more so than youngsters, are able to bridge the gap between abstract facts and increased personal control. More needs to be done to help youngsters understand how to use facts to control outcomes. For instance, college students can learn to use a camera from written instructions. Youngsters may need verbal instructions, demonstrations, and supervised application to control the camera.

Here's an example of using students' desire to control to teach a social studies lesson on gravity:

In addition to receiving a lecture on gravity, students could be asked to look around their homes for heavy objects that are difficult to lift and then design pulleys and levers to lift them (although the actual lifting of these objects should not be a school-sponsored activity). Students will see the direct application of scientific principles to their lives, and also see how those principles improve their own control over the physical objects in their lives.

How many of our children will grow up to become professional basketball or soccer players? Few. It would be far more useful in physical education classes to help students design a physical fitness program they could use throughout their lives, one that would teach them important health lessons and also help them control their weight and conditioning.

Here's another example: A seventh grader named Sara hates the daily lunch menu. There are too few choices, and the choices are often unhealthy. Her English teacher asks the class to identify a problem in the school and then design a procedure to address the problem. Sara launches a letter-writing campaign to the principal, superintendent, and school board to address the problem with school lunches. Her teacher helps her draft the letters and improve the quality of her writing. She is invited to a school board meeting and makes a presentation, thereby honing her public speaking skills. The school board asks her to develop an alternative menu and an accompanying budget, enabling her to learn about the sources and uses of money and also about nutrition. After two months of lobbying Sara is rewarded when the school changes its menu. In addition to the "A" she received from her teacher and the praise she has enjoyed from her schoolmates, Sara has also learned firsthand how to control constructive change.

The control motive is not just a tactic for engaging students directly in academics; it teaches students self-control and the ability to manage their own lives in ways that are productive. It helps young people become responsible for their choices and teaches them to weigh consequences and outcomes. Satisfying the control motive develops lifelong skills that will outlast most of what they will learn from a textbook.

SATISFYING THE CONTROL MOTIVE

Teachers should explain to students how the instruction they are given increases their control of their lives. Knowledge is power if students know how to apply it. Teachers must transform knowledge into know-how by citing applications and giving demonstrations relevant to the students' lives. In this way students will be able to see how learning will increase their control. Students should be prepared and assured that they can achieve each assigned learning objective so they will be confident and ready to extend their control.

The first step in teaching children how to improve their control over what they learn is to teach them to identify their goals and plan a procedure for attaining those goals. This is called behaving purposefully.

Purposeful behavior is:

- Aimed at a specific outcome;

- Based on learning rather than instinct;

- Based on prediction rather than the impulse of the moment or hindsight; and

- Selected by the student rather than predetermined for them.

Students can be taught that by acting purposefully, they are taking an active role in shaping their own destiny, rather than reacting to situations that are imposed on them. When they behave purposefully, they have a much better chance of getting what they want.

The student selects an outcome and identifies a procedure to achieve that outcome. Learning to predict an outcome is, in many cases, a simple process that is already a part of students' lives. For instance, they predict that a glass of water will quench their thirst; that following a particular route will lead to school; that turning the page of a novel will continue the story; that studying will lead to high grades. And they can learn that in unfamiliar situations, research can help them make good predictions. Older students may learn the value of statistical procedures in making accurate predictions.

Let's say a youngster wants to buy a new bicycle. He learns that the bicycle he wants costs $100. He knows that he is paid $20 a week for helping his mother with filing paperwork at her office. He can therefore predict that in five weeks of satisfactory work, he can afford the bicycle. In other words, he has identified an outcome he wants to achieve (I want the bike); he has identified a procedure (working for Mom) that can get him the bike he wants; so he has logically predicted a way to control the outcome.

The same process holds true in the classroom and shows students how learning procedures to achieve a learning objective can help them gain control of their lives. Students can help choose books that interest them for their English classes, they can design methods for testing scientific principles using sports equipment, or they can create a video game that is based on Lewis and Clark's expeditions. In all of these cases, students are using skills needed in their daily lives and designing a procedure to control an outcome. They find these tasks relevant, enjoyable, and empowering.

FOCUSING ON PROCEDURES

In elementary school, students are taught procedures that help them exert control over their lives. They learn language and math skills so they can communicate their needs and desires; they develop physical and social skills that help them influence others and make friends. But in the later grades, students' focus often turns to memorization without applications that are personally meaningful. Research shows that most test items require students to regurgitate facts. Their learning has become removed from their own lives. But students need to learn much more than facts and formulas; they need to learn how to solve problems.

The key to problem solving is developing effective procedures. Students can learn to control outcomes, overcome obstacles, and behave purposefully by creating and executing their own action plans. Productive citizens need to know "how" and "why" as much as "when" and "where." Research shows that the ability to develop procedures to solve problems enhances student achievement. Indeed, these skills are enormously useful beyond the classroom into the world of work and family.

Here is a decision-making procedure students can be taught to solve most problems:

- *Diagnose the problem.* While diagnosing the problem, it's important to define both the current situation and the desired goal so that progress can be accurately planned and monitored. The student must also identify constraints. He must consider his capabilities and the physical and financial limitations on his actions.

For example, Zach, a tenth grader, is getting an "F" in science and wants to get a "B." He has correctly diagnosed a present problem and defined a goal. Now, he must identify a procedure that can raise his grade. His teacher tells him that in order to improve his grade, he must earn a "B" on a science project, improve his performance on weekly quizzes, and earn a "B" on his final exam. All of these factors are within Zach's ability to achieve.

- *Predict solutions.* This involves identifying procedures that have solved similar problems. Schools should show students how to conduct research to find procedures when they don't have them in mind. Accessing information is a key skill that is necessary throughout a person's lifetime. Eventually an older student may learn to create a procedure when research is fruitless. Sometimes the best procedure is to do nothing and let time solve the problem. In Zach's case, research tells him which kinds of science projects earn good grades and win awards. He decides to develop and test an experiment using carbon dioxide gas. He also arranges to be tutored and increases his study time.

- *Implement the plan.* Solutions must be implemented by applying the procedure laid out in the plan. Students may need training on a new procedure or technology. They also need to learn how to estimate whatever resources they will need. Zach conducts his carbon dioxide experiment and writes the results in a research paper. He meets with the tutor and studies more.

- *Assess success.* The student must describe the outcome, and how closely the outcome matched the goal. It's important to note that success on the first try is rare. Rather, success is often achieved after a series of attempts, and students should be encouraged to keep at it. Each time an attempt is made, something new can be learned that makes success on the next attempt more probable. After each unsuccessful attempt the students need to be taught to look for obstacles, refine their procedures, and begin a new cycle. With each successive cycle of problem solving, the students learn something new about how the parts of a process add up to a whole, about behavior and consequences, about a procedure or about their ultimate goal. They must repeatedly revisit their desire to achieve their goal; it may have lost its allure. Initially, the entire process should be kept simple but over time students should learn to predict the effectiveness of complex procedures in achieving solutions, and eventually they should learn to assess side effects and efficiency.

How about our earnest young student, Zach? Has he received his "B"? Was the cost of the tutor worthwhile? Did he learn study skills that can be transferred to other classes? If he correctly diagnosed the problem, created a logical procedure, and executed it, the chances are good that he is celebrating his good grade. And as a bonus, Zach may apply this problem-solving technique to other problems in his life.

SELF-DIRECTED PROBLEM SOLVING

Students can be taught, as they have been for thousands of years, using the Socratic method of asking leading questions to help students find answers. Even better, if young people learn to ask themselves a progression of questions, they will learn to find their own answers. Indeed, students can develop the ability to direct their own, independent learning through self-questioning techniques.

Through self-questioning, students analyze their problem and set a goal, design an efficient, logical sequence of events to achieve the goal, and assess whether the procedure worked. Perhaps the student will realize he needs guidance from his teacher at certain points and learn to ask for help.

Once students become proficient at following instructions to solve problems, they can be taught to use the following simple self-questioning format. It will help them become more self-sufficient, less dependent on their teachers and parents for answers.

- What is my goal? What am I seeking to achieve?
- Are there any constraints?
- Can I recall a procedure I've used in the past to accomplish a similar goal?
- Can I find procedures in the library or on the Internet that have been used to achieve similar goals?
- Which of the procedures do I have the resources and ability to execute?
- Of the procedures I have learned, which is the most likely to succeed?

At the end of this self-questioning, most people will have laid out a roadmap that is practical, efficient, and effective. They learn persistence by refining and reworking their procedure until it is successful. Through self-questioning they discover new resources for answering questions and when to seek assistance in the future.

When students learn to solve problems by designing their own procedures, they get an extra benefit: they learn self-control. The child learns to manage himself and his environment. Most people are intensely interested in controlling their own environment as much as possible—we turn up the heat, we turn on the stove, we turn off the television, we steer the car. Before a person can control outside forces he must first learn to control himself. Through appropriate education, young people learn to examine their own capabilities and interests, set their own goals, and chart their own course.

THE POWER TO INNOVATE

Young people with strong self-discipline and proficiency in problem-solving procedures grow into adults who know how to be innovative. New ideas are fashioned from existing knowledge applied in new ways. Those who know how to identify and manipulate procedures to achieve desired outcomes are well trained to look at existing knowledge with fresh eyes. A person can create a new procedure to achieve a known goal, use an existing procedure to create a new goal, or, if the person is extremely gifted and persistent, create a new procedure to achieve a new goal. In any case, each new innovation allows the innovator and society to exert more control over its environment.

Sometimes these innovations are relatively routine—creating a new recipe, improving a household budget, or writing a short story. And sometimes looking at existing knowledge in a new way can offer breakthroughs, such as airplanes and cures for diseases. These new ideas may apply to procedures, such as a new way to walk to school or a new way to fish, or they may apply to products—new toys, a new article of clothing, a new kind of car, or both—a new procedure to enact new laws.

Most students welcome opportunities to be innovative, if only to break up the monotony of school. They take enormous pleasure in expressing their ideas, in finding ways to conquer challenges. This desire to create is essential to the American character and to the country's continued success in all fields of endeavor. The modern teacher must nurture and channel that desire so that young people can be productive learners throughout their lifetimes.

HIGHLIGHTS

Children are born with a strong desire to learn in order to survive and thrive. Students control what they attend to and learn. Whether they learn a particular lesson depends on whether the presentation captures their interest. Students' interest in the various lessons they are taught can be maintained if they are shown how the lessons improve their control of outcomes. People are almost always motivated to improve their control of their lives. Students' motivation to control can also be engaged by teaching them a generic problem-solving procedure they can use to extend their control in any area and by planning for them to apply the procedure in learning all subjects and in generating innovations, the lifeblood of America's success.

8

Sensible Testing

John Banks had been passing his coursework with flying colors. His father, a school board member, was a staunch advocate of educational improvement and a supporter of the accountability movement—that is, until John failed state accountability tests and was not promoted. John and his family were dumbfounded. How could John and other students they knew who had been routinely promoted suddenly be retained in grade? John's father and parents of many other students who suffered the same fate banded together to protest the destructive impact of accountability testing. Parents who once supported accountability now vehemently opposed it. How could this happen?

Under pressure from employers and the federal government, more than 40 states now have programs to test students in order to qualify them for promotion and graduation, each program with its own criteria, substance, and sanctions. The goal of such testing is to put a stop to the practice of social promotion—promoting students who have not achieved grade-level learning objectives—but the movement has been chaotic and may, in the end, suffocate the strengths of the educational system while trying to fix its weaknesses.

The first accountability programs took hold after World War II, focusing on minority students and those with disabilities. Early efforts dealt with services, such as busing for minorities and Individual Education Plans for the disabled, rather than results. Educators became more indulgent and tended to loosen academic standards for many of these students, and far too many young people were moved through the system without learning minimum skills. In 1997, the federal Americans with Disabilities Act required states to account for the academic achievement of disabled students. Ironically, this act made failing grades even less desirable and increased social promotion. The problem of social promotion was just as serious and widespread in the mainstream student population.

In 2002, President Bush signed the No Child Left Behind Act. This sweeping legislation outlines a detailed roadmap for testing children and holding educators accountable for poor test results, and uses federal money for reading programs and creating charter schools as alternatives for parents whose schools have failed their children. The act requires state standards for reading, math, and, by 2005, science. The act has four main prongs: stronger accountability, more flexibility for states and communities, concentrated resources, and more options for parents.

To employers, who paid millions of dollars and spent countless hours on remedial reading and math programs for job applicants and their employees, the failure of the educational system was painfully obvious. The result—a national testing program—is unprecedented. No nation in the history of the world has embarked on such an enormous undertaking. For the first time, educators are being held directly responsible for the success of their students, and failure to meet this challenge has led to firings and school closings.

Some educators tend to respond to this pressure with excuses: the tests lack validity because they don't test everything the students are taught; too few resources are devoted to the schools; classes are too large; parents are not included in the accountability process, even though they have an enormous effect on learning; students are unmotivated and sometimes disruptive. Although there is some truth in these complaints, they distract from the main point, which is adequacy of instruction.

Testing is not new to educators themselves, who face licensing requirements and school accreditation committees. What is new is that they are now being judged on their students' performance, not theirs. And the judging is being done in public.

EDUCATORS VERSUS STANDARDIZED TESTING

The pressure on educators is therefore enormous, and it is only made worse by the fact that few teachers are trained in achievement test construction. Yet the role of teachers in testing their students is underappreciated. Tests that are constructed by teachers are almost always more valuable at assessing how well their students learn the lessons they teach. Before evaluating the standardized achievement tests, it's important to understand that the traditional method of testing has much to recommend it.

A 1961 study by Bloom and Peters showed that the best way to know how well a young person will do in college is to see how well he or she did in high school. In other words, there is a direct correlation between high school grades and college grades. Therefore, the high school grading system, as disorganized and subjective as it may sometimes be, has actually been reliable over many decades—at least before social promotion became prominent. Another indication of the accuracy of high school grades is research showing that high school class rank is a better predictor of college success than the SAT. Teacher-made tests are intimately connected to what the students are being taught in a way that standardized tests are not.

Since standardized tests are graded based on group norms, and test performance is therefore relative, teacher-made tests are much more useful in determining individual student achievement of class learning objectives and diagnosing the need for corrective instruction. As researchers Salvia and Ysseldyke put it in a 2001 report: "Teachers are the only ones who can match testing and instruction."

Another advantage of teacher-made tests is that the results can be used to help students immediately, whereas standardized test results may not be available for some time. Also, teachers can test what a student has learned in many different ways, such as oral questioning, while standardized tests are largely limited to pencil and paper. Teachers can provide richer feedback than the scorers of a standardized test can. Lastly, many students don't do well under the pressure of timed tests, and some are not accomplished readers.

NUMBERS VERSUS WORDS

One of the greatest debates in educational testing is whether the best test evaluations are those that provide a numerical score or those that use words to evaluate performance. Unfortunately, a schism has developed between the two schools of thought when, in truth, the best kind of test performance evaluation includes both.

Most standardized tests yield quantitative results—in other words, the results of the test are scores. Advocates of numerical scores say this is the most precise way to describe student performance and to grade students. They argue that teachers' comments about their students can be too subjective.

In recent years qualitative evaluations of student performance, such as teacher comments on essays and report cards, have become more popular, in part because educators are seeing the limits of using only test scores to describe student performance. Comments on reports cards are a mixed blessing. They can provide valuable feedback, but they may come too late to keep the student from failing. Instead of helping the student improve, some comments simply provide a rationale to defend the teacher's grade. To prevent classroom failure, teachers must provide their feedback as soon as poor performance is noticed. As more people focus on the importance of providing such feedback, educators are being taught techniques for evaluating students, and some colleges now offer courses in qualitative techniques, which is especially appealing to budding educators who may not be good in math. In fact, a growing number of colleges now offer separate tracks for qualitative and quantitative studies, leading to an unhealthy competition between the two approaches.

The best approach is to start with test scores and add on a layer of analysis from the teacher. Test scores cannot describe the depth and breadth of a student's knowledge. While test scores may indicate a problem, teachers are best prepared to diagnose the cause of the problem and suggest ways of correcting it.

For example, students may be learning about the properties of water. They would learn that about 70 percent of the earth is covered with water (quantitative information) and they may also learn that water is a liquid that people drink and can see through (qualitative information). Water is composed of two parts of hydrogen to one part of oxygen, and must be between 32 degrees and 212 degrees Fahrenheit. In this way, qualitative and quantitative descriptions complement each other to provide a more complete and accurate description.

DIFFERENT KINDS OF TESTING

To say that one type of testing is better than another is a gross oversimplification. Indeed, there are many different kinds of tests that serve different purposes. Too often, tests are used incorrectly.

There are different types of tests used in American schools, each of which performs a unique function.

- *Admission tests*, such as the SAT, determine whether students are ready or qualified for college.

- *Placement tests* are used to evaluate where students should be assigned, such as classes for gifted or developmentally delayed students.

- *Instructional prescription tests* determine how well students have mastered a skill they are being taught, pinpoint deficiencies, and indicate appropriate follow-up instruction.

- *Achievement certification tests* are used to certify achievement of learning objectives and judge whether a student should be promoted to the next grade.

- *Referral tests* can help determine underlying causes of failure to learn, such as poor eyesight, or whether the student has a special vocational interest or talent.

Although some tests are used for more than one purpose—the same test might be used for placement and instruction prescriptions, for instance—most tests are more suited for one type of evaluation. Tests used by educators should not be confused with tests used by school psychologists and other clinicians to determine whether a psychological or physical disorder is underlying student failure.

A major consideration in deciding which test is appropriate is whether the test assesses how well a student has met the criteria for achieving an objective or whether the test assesses where that student stands in relation to a group. Norm-referenced tests are used to judge how a student compares with her peers, by developing group norms and variations. These kinds of tests are most useful when trying to differentiate among students (for example, those seeking scholarships or awards). They are also useful for comparing groups of students (for instance, between states or schools).

Criterion-based tests are used to evaluate how well objectives have been achieved. These kinds of tests are used to judge:

- How well a school meets accountability standards;
- Whether students are ready to be assigned more advanced material;
- Whether students should be promoted to the next grade;
- Whether students should be allowed to graduate; and
- Whether students meet the entry requirements for a school or program.

Which kind of test best serves a given purpose? Again, there is no simple answer. A review of the different kinds of testing shows that both norm-referenced and criterion-referenced testing can be appropriate, depending on the circumstances. Also, the same test can be both norm-referenced and criterion-referenced.

Admission testing. College admission tests have traditionally been norm-referenced, to separate desirable candidates from the pool of applicants. But there is a growing trend toward including qualitative information, such as essays and interviews, to supplement SAT scores and other test scores. In addition, admissions counselors may balance academic test results with a student's involvement in extracurricular activities. Both norm-referenced and criterion-referenced tests are used to judge whether a youngster is ready for first grade. To assess early physical development, children are compared to norms for their age group. Comparing her recitation of the letters to the criterion assesses a child's knowledge of the alphabet: how many of the 26 letters does a child know?

Placement testing. Although a substantial body of research shows that ability grouping does not aid academic achievement, schools still use placement tests to determine whether a student should be assigned to an advanced, regular, or below-average class. Of course, mentally retarded students need to be placed in special education classes designed for them. These tests are usually norm-referenced, in which students are compared with their peers. But there are cases in which a teacher's evaluation makes a difference, such as a recommendation for placement in a class for gifted students.

Instructional prescription testing. The best way to judge how well a student has learned an instructional unit is a teacher-made, criterion-referenced test. Norm-referenced tests do not indicate how well a student has learned a particular lesson and whether he is ready for the next step in an instructional sequence, although they do indicate the grade level at which a student is performing. Teachers prepare each day's lesson, they work with the students in the classroom, and they are in the best position to know whether a student has learned the material. Teachers should provide students with both qualitative and quantitative feedback. It's especially useful if students are asked to explain their answers on a test, so the teacher can see how well the student has learned the material. Teachers must be provided with training on how to construct achievement tests, however.

Achievement certification testing. At the heart of the accountability testing movement is achievement certification testing, which is used to decide whether students should be promoted or allowed to graduate. In a number of states, norm-referenced tests are used to combat social promotions. But norm-referenced testing does not adequately assess whether a student has met learning objectives. For example, norm-referenced tests are used to grade on a curve, making it possible for a student to perform better than most of his peers and earn an "A" on the test and still not have mastered the material. Only criterion-referenced tests are appropriate to judge the extent to which a student has achieved a learning objective. Still, the problem of social promotion is a stubborn one and has been worsened by teachers' lack of knowledge about how to construct an achievement test. In general, teachers need more training in constructing achievement tests, and only tests that accurately assess grade-level achievement should be used for deciding whether a student should be promoted.

Instructional prescription tests and achievement tests are not to be confused. Instructional prescription tests are constructed by teachers to be administered at the end of a lesson; then teachers prescribe the next lesson based on the test results. Review lessons are prescribed when the results reveal that learning is insufficient. Otherwise the teachers prescribe and present the next more advanced lesson.

Achievement certification tests are standardized achievement tests, designed to certify grade level of student achievement. Experts in standardized achievement test construction should construct these tests. Most teachers are not qualified as yet.

Referral testing. In this case, criterion-referenced testing is normally used. Most often, student referrals for further testing are based on comparisons between student performance and criteria of adequate performance, not on group norms. The important factor is whether the student falls below the level of adequate performance. Norms need to be used to assess certain deficiencies, however. For instance, age norms are used to assess physical development in early childhood.

Some published tests, such as the Stanford Achievement Tests, are both norm- and criterion-referenced. In these cases, census data is used to establish national norms, factoring in such variables as socioeconomic and urban-rural status. School curricula are reviewed to develop criteria that are common across districts, and test items are developed to assess knowledge of common subject matter. In this case, however, the tests may not sufficiently represent what was taught at a particular school.

Often, a teacher will use several different types of tests to judge whether a student has mastered material. Many students perform better on one kind of test than on another. Although many educators prefer the classic pencil-and-paper test because it's easy to administer and grade, some students don't do well on these kinds of tests. Timed written tests are especially stressful for some young people. Some students may need more time to perform a task or might do better with an oral exam. Timing a test is usually more useful for the test administrator than for the student. After all, what matters is how well a student knows the material, not how quickly he can finish a test. Indeed, the biggest difference in students' ability is not whether they can learn material but how much instruction they need to master it.

Multiple kinds of testing can also help teachers pinpoint the cause of a student's failures, offering more complete diagnostic information. Diagnostic information is essential if a teacher is designing corrective instruction for a student.

Students with defined disabilities are often allowed to take tests that are tailored to their disabilities. Students who do not qualify for extra assistance under the Americans with Disabilities Act should be entitled to the same opportunity to show what they have learned in a format that is most accommodating to them.

TEST CONSTRUCTION

Think of a test as a tool, like a screwdriver or a computer. Its primary use in education is to assess academic achievement. Like a screwdriver, it must be effective and appropriate, and the instructions for administering the test must be clearly understandable. In testing lingo, a test must be reliable, valid, and objective. (For more on reliability, validity, and objectivity, see Chapter 3.)

Every test needs all three components—reliability, validity, and objectivity—although there is a fair amount of disagreement among test experts about their definitions and applications. In fact, the disagreement over test definitions doesn't bode well for testing as an industry. It's imperative that test experts use terms that are relevant to education and meaningful to educators.

Many educators have a hard time relating the priorities of test experts to their classrooms. For instance, the concept of objectivity tends to become a footnote to the test experts while to teachers, objectivity is of greater importance in the classroom, since teachers must defend against accusations of subjectivity to irate students, parents, elected officials, and attorneys.

Another problem for teachers and parents is that statistics are used extensively by national test publishers in developing standardized, norm-referenced tests. Unfortunately, some of those tests take on a mathematical life of their own, divorced from the context of educators and the essence of instructional programs that the test is supposed to measure. When this happens, tests lose their usefulness.

CHOOSING THE RIGHT TEST

To understand whether a school is properly testing its students, it's important to understand the right way to choose a test. The first step is defining the population to be tested and the characteristics to be observed within that population. That may be as simple as specifying math achievement of third graders. A clear definition helps when choosing the right testing tool.

The next step is to identify tests that describe the characteristics of your target population. Most test manuals and reviews specify the population for which the test is intended, and manuals also specify the characteristics assessed by the test. More than one test might be needed or appropriate for the population being tested.

The educator then selects from among the identified tests those that are reliable, valid, and objective. The first priority should be validity. Reliability and objectivity are also important, but first and foremost the test must be valid. Educators should look for tests with substantial evidence of validity, even if evidence of reliability and objectivity is less overwhelming.

Finally, the educator selects the test that is most feasible to obtain, administer, score, and interpret. Feasibility is an often-overlooked aspect of testing. The amount of time educators can allocate to testing is limited. Teachers have too little time for instruction to begin with, and that time is easily eroded by peripheral responsibilities such as collecting permission slips, lunch duty, photocopying, preparing extracurricular activities, and so on. The temptation can exist to lean on published group tests rather than creating a whole new test for a class. Teachers must receive adequate training, support, and time for developing and administering tests that are directly relevant to their classwork.

Once the appropriate test is chosen, it must be administered properly. The test must be given correctly and the test results must be tallied accurately. Furthermore, the testing conditions must be appropriate—the environment needs to be comfortable and free of distractions, the lighting must be adequate, and the students must have the right supplies for taking the test.

GRADING STUDENTS

Substantial research shows that teacher expectation of students affects the grades they assign, no matter how hard a teacher tries to remain unbiased. When teachers expect individual students to perform well, they grade them according to that expectation, and the same holds true for students who are expected to perform poorly. If a student receives a low or failing grade, parents should understand the process by which that grade was assigned to ensure that the grade is based on fact, not fantasy.

The best way for educators to prevent charges of unfairness is to draw up grading criteria that are shared with the entire class at the beginning of the term, including listing the tests, projects, and other assignments that will be calculated in the grade. Each student should know the maximum number of points that can be earned in a term and how those points are converted into grades. For instance, 90 percent or more of maximum points would be equivalent to an "A"; 80 percent to 89 percent, a "B"; 70 percent to 79 percent, a "C"; 60 percent to 69 percent, a "D"; and below 60 percent, an "F." Establishing criteria at the beginning of the term helps maintain objectivity and allows teachers to better defend their grading decisions at the end of the term.

Using several different methods of judging student performance—tests, essays, projects—to develop one aggregate grade can effectively illustrate how well a child has done in a class. Educators can decide the different types of tests and projects that will be used to reach a grade, but the best approach overall is a formula that is simple, logical, plausible, and has some precedent. This kind of system is easily understood by both students and parents, it follows a coherent format, and it rewards students for their actual performance. Such a system is especially defensible if it has been used by other educators or over time, so that it has been tested and found reasonable.

Pedro is in the third grade, where his favorite subject is math. At the beginning of the quarter, the teacher told Pedro's class that the math grade would be composed of weekly quizzes, a monthly test, and two special projects. Each project was worth 20 points for a total of 40, the tests were worth 10 points each for a total of 30, and the weekly quizzes were worth 2.5 points each for a total of 30. In this way, the teacher showed the students that the special projects required a great deal of attention but that if they did well every week, their grade would reflect their mastery of the subject. Pedro got a total of 86 for a grade of "B," which he and his family fully understood and accepted since they understood how the grades were derived.

PORTFOLIO TESTING

Another trend in testing is portfolio assessment. Many students fare poorly on pencil-and-paper tests that are rigidly timed, so in states such as Vermont, Kentucky, California, and Pennsylvania, teachers have been encouraged to collect student work in portfolios. A wide variety of work can make its way into a child's portfolio, including classroom assignments, a list of books that have been read, checklists, journal entries, artwork, and videos. In addition to the individual student's work, the portfolio might include group assignments. Portfolios have traditionally been used in fields such as art, music, photography, journalism, and modeling, but now they are also used to document academic work over time as well.

What to include in a portfolio and how to judge its contents have been difficult to standardize. Teachers have sometimes been urged to allow students to set their own performance standards, and some educators advocate including students, classmates, parents, and other family members among those who assess portfolios.

Without using specific criteria to guide the evaluation of portfolio material, the assessment is prone to inaccurate scoring. Furthermore, the material in the portfolio may bear little relationship to what was actually taught in the classroom. Portfolios are, in other words, not valid, reliable, or objective as a testing method. Researchers McLoughlin and Lewis argued in 2001 that portfolios are especially unhelpful in predicting future success in school and life beyond school.

Deriving an aggregate score from a portfolio is practically impossible. For example, let's say a student has 16 items in a portfolio prepared for a zoology course. The portfolio contains a videotape on cats; two papers about snakes; six journal entries on the student's reactions to birds; reports on frogs, lizards, and salamanders; pictures of a field trip to a zoo; and an essay written with another student about evolution. Each element of the portfolio is given a score. How does the teacher combine the scores to assign a grade? Assigning different weights to different elements will result in different grades. Including team projects is especially problematic, since the work of the individual student is invisible.

As Salvia and Ysseldyke reported in 2001, "Currently, there appears to be more conviction than empirical support for the use of portfolios. Even given the most optimistic interpretation of the validity of portfolio assessment, we believe that the current literature provides an insufficient basis for an acceptance of portfolio assessment on any basis other than experimental."

There is nothing wrong with assembling samples of student work, and it is possible to create a portfolio assessment system that is reliable, valid, and objective. Unfortunately, most uses of portfolios today can't be defended as reliable, valid, and objective.

STUDENTS' POTENTIAL

For decades, American educators have been under the illusion that aptitude testing can ascertain a student's potential—how a student will perform in the future. Aptitude tests are an industry unto themselves; the SAT for those seeking college admission, the Vane Kindergarten Test, the Stanford-Binet Intelligence Test. Educators are constantly assessing a student's potential and using those assessments for academic placement.

Yet there is reason to reconsider traditional concepts and definitions about academic aptitude. One of the most enlightening definitions was written by John Carroll in 1963: Aptitude is the amount of time needed to learn a task under optimal conditions. Students with greater aptitude learn faster and with less instruction. Carroll has also shown that virtually all students can achieve learning objectives through high school, given adequate time and instruction. Therefore, under ideal conditions where all students are given sufficient instruction, there should be little difference in academic achievement through high school. Under this scenario, academic potential is really an irrelevant concept.

Aptitude tests were originally intended to distinguish mentally challenged students needing special education from the main population, but that original purpose has been distorted. The Stanford-Binet Intelligence Test has been used to assess academic potential for many years. It is most effective in identifying mentally retarded students, and low scores on the Binet test are accurate for that purpose. But higher Binet scores are not nearly as useful in identifying students with exceptionally high potential for achievement. For instance, someone who scores high on the Binet may not necessarily succeed in business or make any great discoveries or create any new inventions.

Indeed, the line between aptitude testing, which purports to look ahead, and academic achievement testing, which analyzes the present, is quite fuzzy. As researchers Frankel and Wallen wrote in 1996: "Aptitude tests are intended to measure an individual's potential to achieve; in actuality, they measure present skills and abilities. . . . The same test may be either an aptitude or achievement test depending on the purpose for which it is used. A mathematics test, for example, may also measure aptitude for additional mathematics." In scoring such tests, it can become difficult to evaluate which scores relate to potential and which scores relate to current knowledge.

Those who place a lot of weight on IQ scores are similarly misguided. The Binet test that results in an IQ score assumes that IQ remains stable over time. But that stability is simply a function of the formula used to derive a score. One formula divides a person's achievement test score by his chronological age. Achievement scores in the numerator are devised to increase proportionately with age in the denominator, keeping the IQ similar year after year. The test items on pencil-and-paper IQ tests are similar to the test items on achievement tests. In the final analysis, the IQ test is fairly ineffective for anything other than identifying mental deficiency.

For all the money that has been poured into aptitude testing and all the resultant anxiety, the cheapest and most accurate way to assess student academic potential is simply on the basis of their previous record. No additional testing should be necessary. (The only exception is for preschoolers who do not have sufficient academic records, and even then, other criteria such as social and self-care skills also need to be considered to assess potential for success in school.) Rather than continue to search for new ways to peek at student potential, more can be gained by finding new ways to use existing academic records.

The purpose of the following list is to familiarize advocates and others interested in education with some of the tests that young people might be asked to take:

- *Admission to grade school*: These tests are used to assess children's readiness to enter school for the first time. Preschool Language Scale, Bracken Basic Concept Scale, Mullen Scales of Early Learning, Early Childhood Behavior Scale, Preschool Evaluation Scale, Boehm Test of Basic Concepts, Metropolitan Readiness Test, Developmental Indicators for the Assessment of Learning, Cognitive Skills Assessment Battery.

- *Admission to college*: PSAT, SAT, ACT, GRE, LSAT.

- *Placement tests*: These tests are used to place individuals in appropriate programs, schools, or classes. Stanford-Binet Intelligence

Scale, Wechsler Adult Intelligence Scale, Wechsler Intelligence Scale for Children, Leiter International Performance Scale, Peabody Picture Vocabulary Test, Universal Nonverbal Intelligence Test, Test of Nonverbal Intelligence, Otis-Lennon School Ability Test, Detroit Tests of Learning Aptitude, Naglieri Nonverbal Ability Test, Clinical Evaluation of Language Fundamentals, Wide Range Assessment of Memory and Learning, Kaufman Assessment Battery for Children, Screening Assessment for Gifted Elementary Students, Cognitive Assessment System, Woodcock-Johnson Psychoeducation Battery, Brigance Screens, Diagnostic Achievement Battery.

- *Instructional prescription tests*: These tests diagnose academic inadequacies as a basis for prescribing appropriate corrective instruction.

  Instructional prescription tests for math: Stanford Diagnostic Math Test, Key Math Revised, Test of Mathematical Abilities, Test of Early Mathematics Ability, STAR Math Test.

  Instructional prescriptions tests for reading: Early Reading Diagnostic Assessment, Gray Oral Reading Test, Stanford Diagnostic Reading Test, Test of Early Reading Ability, Woodcock Reading Mastery Tests, Standardized Reading Inventory.

  Instructional prescription tests for spoken and written language: Comprehensive Receptive and Expressive Vocabulary Test, Test of Adolescent Language, Test of Auditory Comprehension of Language, Test of Early Language Development, Test of Early Written Language, Test of Written Language, Test of Handwriting Skills, Comprehensive Assessment of Spoken Language, Test of Written Spelling.

- *Achievement certification tests*: These tests are used to certify level of academic achievement. California Achievement Test, Iowa Tests of Educational Development, Iowa Tests of Basic Skills, Metropolitan Achievement Tests, Terra Nova Test, Peabody Individual Achievement Test, Kaufman Test of Educational Achievement, Mini-Battery of Achievement Tests, Stanford Achievement Test Series, Wide Range Achievement Test, General Education Development Test (GED).

- *Referral tests*: These tests are used to diagnose underlying causes of failure to learn.

  Referral tests for personal problem evaluation: Adaptive Behavior Scale, Adaptive Behavior Assessment System, Vineland Adaptive Behavior Scale, Devereux Behavior Rating Scale, Developmental Test of Visual Perception, Visual Skills Appraisal, Developmental Test of Visual-Motor Integration, Test of Gross Motor Development, Test of Auditory-Perceptual Skills.

Referral tests for vocational guidance: The Harrington–O'Shea Career Decision-Making System, Strong Interest Inventory, Occupational Attitude Survey and Interest Schedule, Kuder Occupational Interest Survey.

Here are some resources for test evaluations and more information about testing:

- *Educators' Handbook on Effective Testing* (Friedman et al., 2003).
- *A Consumer's Guide to Tests in Print* (2nd ed.) (Hammill, Brown, & Bryant, 1992).
- *Tests: A Comprehensive Reference for Assessments in Psychology, Education, and Business* (3rd ed.) (Sweetland & Keyser, 1991).
- The Buros Institute Mental Measurement Yearbooks (www.ericaenet/testcol.htm).

MISGUIDED TESTING

It seems to serve the purpose of many professionals to argue that teachers can't construct valid, reliable, and objective tests. Psychometricians—those who study the science of mental measurement—say teachers don't know enough about statistics to competently design tests. These arguments elevate the status of psychometricians at the expense of teachers, and needlessly so. While most teachers and school administrators would be the first to agree that teachers lack expertise and time, the fact remains that tests developed by classroom teachers are the most accurate way of assessing classroom learning. Teachers do need to learn more about constructing achievement tests and defending the administration and conclusions of their tests. Under no circumstances should teachers abandon the achievement-testing field to the test experts.

Unfortunately, the purpose of educational testing has been obscured over the years by political agendas and other noneducational priorities. The primary goal of achievement testing should be to indicate the instruction needed to facilitate academic success, plain and simple. But the drive for national standardized testing has created a multibillion-dollar industry often run by educational outsiders whose experience lies in psychometrics rather than teaching. The result has been, too often, that an industrial tail is wagging the education dog. The standardized tests become the school curriculum.

Tests that try to serve the purposes of all educators may serve the purposes of none. Basing grades, promotions, and graduations on test results that are relative—that is, norm-referenced—is indefensible. National normed achievement tests may be useful in comparing the performance of groups and group members, but they cannot be used to judge individuals' achievement of class learning objectives.

Worse, these tests are being used in ways that they were not designed for. To use one test score for admissions, placement, or any other kind of decision about an individual student is seriously misguided. Accountability testing is used to judge teachers and administrators as well as students.

Accountability is here to stay, though, and it's long overdue. The process must focus on individual schools and individual teachers. Teachers whose students consistently fail these tests must be given more training, but if the students keep failing, the teachers must be replaced. In today's world it is easier to fire a teacher for offensive language than for incompetence. Administrators should also be judged on the success of the students in their schools. Administrators must focus on providing competent teachers to teach students who are ready to learn the material.

Educators and parents must also get involved in the evolving world of testing to ensure that the new accountability movement doesn't crush initiative and talent. Some states have extended their testing program far beyond simply accurately assessing whether students meet minimum standards. This process has curbed educators' discretion and initiative in unwelcome ways. Teachers and administrators should be encouraged to go beyond meeting minimum standards to enrich their students' educations. Instead, in far too many places, teachers are forced to "teach to the test," throttling academic freedom and reducing enrichment activities.

In the frenzy to stop social promotion, the majority of students may be getting a less enriched education than previously. All students should be given the opportunity to achieve their fullest potential, but the new focus on test-taking skills and rote learning is actually a step backward. States should be testing for basic knowledge and then allowing teachers the freedom to work with their students in creative ways. Innovation is at the core of America's success; students need to learn more than the basics to ensure the country's future success. It is both unnecessary and harmful for these accountability tests to become the standards for America's educational system.

It took decades for the brunt of social promotion to be felt. There are no records of social promotion. It was not until the job market was flooded with illiterate and undereducated job applicants and industry was forced into literacy training to fill minimum job requirements that the business world took action. Their powerful lobbies caused state legislatures to enact accountability testing laws. State education agencies were exposed and embarrassed and, in a frenzy to comply, many overreacted. They went into the test construction business full-scale and attempted to test student learning of almost everything taught in the state.

The consequences of accountability testing overkill are enormous. Severe penalties are mandated against educators when too many of their students do not pass the test. Teachers in fear of losing their jobs feel coerced to teach to the test. The tests are so comprehensive that very little teaching time is left for teacher initiative and enrichment. The tests oppress educators and increase testing time during the school year substantially, leaving less time for teaching.

Enforcing accountability legislation does serve to curtail social promotion, but it also increases the failure rate considerably. Underachieving students who would have been promoted in the past do not pass the tests and are no longer promoted. To make certain that incompetent students are not promoted, some states not only closed loopholes, they raised test standards for promotion, which further increases the failure rate. And an increase in the failure rate can be expected to increase the dropout rate because dropouts typically fail in school before they drop out.

As time passes, more and more students fail the tests. Their parents don't understand why their child, who had been promoted routinely, suddenly became a failure. Teachers who are sanctioned because too many of their students fail the tests do not understand why their competence is suddenly being questioned. Consequently, parents and teachers are outraged and joining together to challenge the validity of the tests and protest the destructive effects of accountability testing.

Social promotion can be stopped without going overboard. Commercially available, nationally standardized achievement tests have been perfected over many years. Most states are familiar with them and have used them. They assess student achievement in all the subjects commonly taught across the United States in as little as six hours. Setting minimum standards for passing the tests will ensure that incompetent students are not promoted without unnecessarily failing students. These tests are quite comprehensive, even though they do not assess achievement of all of the idiosyncratic learning objectives pursued in any given state. (Many of these tests were mentioned by name on page 92 under the heading "*Achievement certification tests.*")

The proposed achievement testing plan will reduce expenses, the failure rate, testing time, parent and teacher dissatisfaction, and the need for states to be in the test construction business. It will increase educator and student morale as well as time available for instruction and enrichment in the classroom. In addition, nationally standardized tests allow test performance of students, schools, and states to be compared across America.

For education to be effective, more of the decisions made by educators must be based on scientific evidence. Presenting evidence to educators in plain English will go a long way to bridge the gap between research and practice. It's also important to focus research on central rather than peripheral issues. The most central issue is the cause–effect relationship between instruction and desired learning, since instruction is primarily responsible for instilling desired learning. The general research question to be addressed is: What kind of instruction produces what kind of learning in what kind of student? To illustrate more specifically, does the Horton Reading Instruction Program increase reading achievement in third graders?

Excessive moralistic pronouncements of right and wrong actions often interfere with evidence-based decision-making, as does fear of litigation. For example, teachers no longer make physical contact with children for fear that they may be accused of immoral or illegal behavior. Not too long ago teachers physically stopped one student from assaulting another and punished disruptive students with the proverbial ruler on occasion, but no more.

Certainly, education is a moral responsibility and must proceed according to law. Still, instructional techniques that are proven effective and legal to use are prevented from being adopted because educators who have the say-so question the morality of putting them into practice.

Educators tend to be highly moral. Most sacrifice income to become educators, taking the moral high ground by teaching our children to become law-abiding, productive citizens. Too often, however, they prevent legal interventions proven to work from being adopted by raising doubts about the morality of the practice. Is it right for kids? Ought we treat kids that way? Should we teach that to children?

Morality and scientific progress often clash. We have been pondering the morality of applications of nuclear energy and genetic engineering for some time. They prompt legal interpretations from our judiciary and the enactment of new laws by legislatures. As citizens we are committed to abide by the law, but not by additional moral edicts. The number of laws keeps increasing because more laws are enacted than deleted. Heaping moral edicts and "political correctness" on top of legal edicts can become adversely restrictive. Every effort must be made to abide by the law in education and to keep additional moral edicts from banning the adoption of scientific advancements in our schools.

Finally, parents, school board members, politicians, and other citizens that actively affect education must not allow themselves to become disoriented. The one and only goal of education is and always has been to instill desired learning. It is their job to specify as policy objectives the desired learning schools must instill. Educators are not better qualified to determine the policy objectives students need to achieve to become productive citizens, workers, and family members, although many educators may think otherwise.

Educators are better prepared to determine the means of achieving the policy objectives (curriculum and instruction). However, they often lose sight of their reason for being and stray off course, as well intended as they may be.

HIGHLIGHTS

Achievement testing is the most prevalent testing educators do. It is used to (1) assess achievement, (2) derive grades, and (3) prescribe instruction. Diagnostic testing is done primarily by clinicians to diagnose and treat underlying causes of failure to learn. Teachers need to be better prepared to construct achievement tests they need to assess student learning of the subjects they teach. Teacher-made tests can be more accurate in assessing achievement of a school's objectives than standardized tests. Criteria-referenced achievement tests are more relevant to assessing the achievement of instructional objectives than norm-referenced tests. Although grades should be based on the results of multiple testing, portfolio testing leaves much to be desired. Aptitude tests are more accurate in revealing students' limitations than their superiority. Although accountability testing is needed to prevent social promotion, it should not be overdone. Social promotion can be prevented using published tests that can be administered in as little as six hours.

9

Key Scientific Facts

Education is not nearly as effective as it could be. Many practices shown by research to work haven't been adopted in our schools. Furthermore, practices that research has shown for some time do not work continue to be used in many American schools. Following are important scientific facts about educational practices that serve to highlight and verify many of the statements made earlier. The facts also provide a basis for initiating immediate educational reform. (Suggestions are provided in Chapter 10.) References appear at the end of this book so that additional information can be obtained. Keep in mind that scientific facts are not absolute; they are based on results of numerous studies that verify a fact at a high level of probability.

1. All but the most psychologically handicapped students can achieve all of the learning objectives required through high school.
2. The difference among students is the amount of instruction they may need to achieve the learning objectives.

John Carroll spent most of his career verifying these two facts. To establish the facts he continued to provide instruction for failing students until they qualified for promotion and graduation. Benjamin Bloom (1968) further verified these facts. A compelling amount of research shows that the quantity of instruction students receive is largely responsible for their success in school. Bloom extended his research into the quality of instruction, and consequently derived Mastery Learning. Mastery Learning instruction ensures that students are given all the instruction they need to succeed. In addition, it incorporates a number of techniques that have been proven to advance learning. His disciples J. H. Block and Lorin Anderson (1975) provided practical applications of Mastery Learning to classroom instruction.

Benjamin Bloom (1984), A. J. Burke (1983), and J. Anania (1981) in separate studies analyzed a large amount of data to demonstrate that

3. One-on-one tutoring is much more effective than classroom instruction in increasing student achievement.

The following instructional strategies have been shown to increase academic achievement. They are described by Myles Friedman in *Ensuring Student Success* (2000). Detailed research support for the strategies is presented in his *Handbook on Effective Instructional Strategies* (1998). Over 1,700 research studies are cited in the handbook. From 50 to over 200 studies support each of the strategies to be described.

Defining Instructional Expectations
Number of supportive studies: 169
4. (1) Learning objectives, (2) procedures used to achieve them, and (3) the criteria used to judge their achievement must be spelled out for students before instruction begins.

Taking Student Readiness into Account
Number of supportive studies: 171
5. Lessons should be based on evidence of students' readiness to learn them.

Providing Effective Instructional Evaluation
Number of supportive studies: 219
6. Instruction and certification of student achievement must be based on accurate evaluation of student performance.

Providing Corrective Instruction
Number of supportive studies: 219
7. Students' achievement is increased when corrective instruction is administered to correct their mistakes.

Providing Contiguity
Number of supportive studies: 178
8. The understanding of relationships is enhanced when to-be-related

events are presented close together in time and space (using such aids as maps, time-lapse photography, and planetariums).

Utilizing Repetition Effectively
Number of supportive studies: 68
9. Repetition in the presentation of information and in practicing skills enhances learning.

Clarifying Communication
Number of supportive studies: 111
10. For students to learn information it must be clearly communicated to them.

Providing Unifiers
Number of supportive studies: 50
11. Unifying schemes such as topic outlines and graphs enhance the learning of complex relationships.

Keeping Students on Task
Number of supportive studies: 64
12. Students learn more when they stay focused on assigned tasks.

Providing Ample Teaching Time
Number of supportive studies: 63
13. Learning increases when teachers spend more time teaching during class sessions.

Providing Ample Learning Time
Number of supportive studies: 168
14. Learning is enhanced when students are given the time they need to complete assignments.

Utilizing Reminders
Number of supportive studies: 79
15. Recall of information is enhanced when memory joggers such as Post-It notes are used to cue the recall of the information.

Providing Transfer of Learning Instruction
Number of supportive studies: 73
16. Achievement is enhanced when students are taught a procedure for applying learning to the solution of present problems.

Providing Decision-Making Instruction
Number of supportive studies: 79

17. Problem solving is enhanced when students are taught a procedure for making accurate decisions.

Facilitating Teamwork
Number of supportive studies: 165
18. Achievement is enhanced when students cooperate to solve problems.

Reducing Student/Teacher Ratio Below 15 to 1
Number of supportive studies: 101
19. Classroom learning increases as student/teacher ratio decreases below 15 to 1. Any decrease from a higher ratio to 15 to 1 does not significantly increase learning. Generally speaking, public schools have not been able to afford a student/teacher ratio reduction below 15 to 1 in their regular classrooms.

Here are effective practices that have been supported by many but fewer than 50 research studies. Caroline Evertson (1995) conducted a number of studies during her distinguished career that support the following:

20. Classroom disruptions are reduced when teachers specify a few rules of conduct and consequences for violating them on the first class meeting, and enforce the rules soon after violations occur.

Sigmund Freud emphasized the importance of early learning on later life. Bloom (1964) analyzed a massive amount of data to show that:

21. The amount of learning that takes place during the first five years of life far exceeds the amount of learning that occurs in any comparable time period.
22. Far fewer students are victims of violent crimes in school than away from school.

COMMON PRACTICES THAT DON'T WORK

Following are common practices that have been used and studied for some time. There is no evidence to support their continued use.

23. Research does not show that in-school suspension, out-of-school suspension, expulsion, or counseling make violent students less violent.

24. There is no evidence indicating that teachers with particular personal characteristics are more effective in producing student achievement. (Effective teaching results from learning and applying effective teaching techniques.)

25. Evidence confirms that whole language instruction is not an effective method of teaching language.

26. Research verifies that ability grouping does not enhance student achievement.

27. Research shows that reinforcement does not increase academic achievement.

Practices 23–27 should be discontinued.

10

Gateways to Achievement

Great strides can be made in reducing the failure rate by advancing (1) teacher and administrator preparation and (2) preventive tutoring.

TEACHER AND ADMINISTRATOR PREPARATION

To improve teacher and administrator pre-service and in-service preparation, the focus must be on (1) teaching proficiency and (2) teaching evaluation.

Teaching Proficiency

To become more proficient, teachers must be taught how to use instructional strategies that have been proven to increase student achievement and to construct more accurate achievement tests to assess student achievement.

Teaching can certainly be improved if teachers and prospective teachers are taught to utilize the 20 effective instructional strategies previously discussed.

Being able to apply proven instructional strategies is necessary for proficient teaching, but it is not sufficient. In addition, teachers must be able to assess their students' progress in learning the lessons they teach and to diagnose learning inadequacies as a basis for prescribing corrective instruction. Students seldom master skills they are taught on their first attempt; teachers must be able to diagnose inadequacies from the mistakes students make on class tests and assignments as a basis for reteaching lessons that students are having difficulty with. In short, teachers need to be proficient in constructing the kinds of achievement tests they need to assess student learning of the lessons they teach. They also need to be taught how to score and aggregate scores on class tests and assignments to assign grades, and how to interpret results of standardized tests commonly used in education. Standardized tests can help teachers and administrators to assess student progress and inadequacies.

Unfortunately, most teacher preparation programs do not provide sufficient instruction in achievement testing. Teachers have not been prepared and certified to construct accurate achievement tests. Pre-service and in-service teacher preparation must redress the neglect. Teacher-made tests need not be inferior to standardized tests; they can be superior in assessing achievement of classroom objectives. Standardized achievement tests are constructed to assess what is commonly taught across the United States and may not sufficiently measure the curriculum taught in particular classes and schools. With the appropriate instruction, teachers can learn how to construct and defend their achievement tests and test results with confidence to students, parents, and grievance committees, and in courts of law.

Teaching Evaluation

The focus needs to be on teaching evaluation instead of teacher evaluation. There has been a sizable amount of research on teacher traits, such as knowledge and personality, but there is no evidence proving that teacher traits are linked with an increase in academic achievement. On the other hand, all of the effective teaching strategies discussed earlier have been shown to increase student achievement. These strategies can be learned, evaluated, and perfected.

The key to student success is perfecting teaching based on observations and evaluations of teaching performance. Teaching cannot be evaluated using pencil-and-paper tests, oral exams, interviews, or peer or student opinion. Teaching can only be evaluated through observation of teachers or teachers-in-training in the act of teaching students. Teaching evaluation might take place in a classroom or a tutoring session, either actual or simulated. Evaluators might be present or behind a one-way mirror, or a videotape of an earlier session might be used.

Since research shows that teaching techniques rather than teacher traits are responsible for increasing academic achievement, it is folly to focus on teacher evaluation. Teachers with odd traits can be very proficient at teaching. Moreover, it is all too easy to neglect teaching evaluation in favor of teacher evaluation. More teachers may have been dismissed because of bizarre or submoral behavior than because of poor teaching. Finally, most personal traits may not be alterable through teacher education.

Although hardly anyone enjoys being evaluated, teaching evaluation tends to be less personally threatening and more productive than teacher evaluation. The focus is on routinely improving the teaching skills of all teachers, not on a personal makeover. Screening of applicants for teaching can ensure that the vast majority who are hired do not have problems that impair teaching; for instance, a serious speech impediment.

PREVENTIVE TUTORING

The purpose of preventive tutoring is to prevent failure. It needs to be provided because (1) most students can succeed given sufficient instruction, (2) one-to-one tutoring is much more effective than classroom instruction, and (3) teachers do not have sufficient time during class to give all students all the personal instruction they need to succeed. Preventive tutoring is provided outside of class by volunteers such as parents and retirees and as needed by hired tutors. Student assignment to special education classes or teachers is not required. In fact, preventive tutoring reduces the number of students that need special education.

Preventive tutoring is coordinated with classroom teachers who show tutors the mistakes students are making on class tests and assignments that need to be corrected. Tutors use class textbooks and materials as a basis for understanding and reteaching topics students are having difficulty learning. Tutors are chosen who know the topic and then oriented to their assignment. Only part-time tutors are needed.

The focus of educators must be on teaching and evaluating individual students rather than classes. It is individual students, not classes, who earn grades and promotion. To succeed in school, students must be given as much instruction as they need. Classes may be taught and class averages may be useful, but classes are not assigned grades or refused promotion.

Delivering Preventive Tutoring

At first there is no need to hire someone to oversee preventive tutoring. The special education teachers in charge of the resource rooms are well qualified. They are well qualified to administer tutoring, as well as tests to diagnose academic inadequacies. They are also able to refer students to clinical specialists for diagnosis and treatment of underlying causes of failure to learn, such as vision, hearing, motor, and attention deficits. The special education teacher's supervisory responsibilities can be extended to include preventive tutoring, given assistance as needed. Tutoring is not only provided for in the Individuals with Disabilities Education Act for disabled students; it is also provided for in the No Child Left Behind Act for students failing class assignments who are not disabled. Although money is always in short supply, funds are available to provide tutoring for needy students. A substantial reduction in the failure rate is all the justification that is needed for additional funding.

Preventive tutoring should be initiated by classroom teachers who might be more enthusiastic about working with a tutoring program, now that there is so much pressure on them to increase student achievement. They would refer students having difficulty with lessons currently being taught to the resource room teachers. The resource room teacher provides a tutor and tutoring space and serves as liaison between tutors and classroom teachers. The tutor receives the students' low test and class assignment scores and other materials that can be used as guides for tutoring. Tutors continue to provide tutoring until the students master topics sufficiently to progress with their classmates, or the resource room teacher determines that the student needs to receive special education or to be referred to a clinician to diagnose underlying causes of failure to learn.

Once students referred for preventive tutoring are being successfully tutored, the tutoring services can be extended as desired. For instance, other students can be encouraged to volunteer for preventive tutoring when they are having difficulty with classroom topics. Marginal students earning "D" grades in a subject know when they are in need of help. Allowing voluntary access to preventive tutoring can further reduce the failure rate. Furthermore, it reduces the stigma of being tutored. If all students have free access to tutoring and take advantage of it, being tutored is less embarrassing.

Eventually, as an ideal, it might be best for students if schools had mastery centers instead of resource rooms. Mastery centers have an open-door policy. All students who come to a mastery center to learn are given personal attention, even if they are doing well in school and are simply seeking enrichment. It may be that the best way to serve the needs of talented and gifted students is through individualized guidance. After all, classroom instruction, by its very nature, imposes conformity—at least conformity to class rules and requirements. Innovations need to be nurtured: American industry thrives on innovation. Students would clamor to take advantage of a mastery center that helps any student learn any subject they need or want to learn.

In summary, to prevent failure it is necessary to provide preventive tutoring for students who have received failing scores on class tests and assignments. When feasible, tutoring can be extended to include volunteers who want help learning topics they are taught in class. Finally, tutoring and advisement can be extended to successful students who want to pursue their personal interests. Curiosity and ambition are too valuable to waste.

COST/EFFECTIVENESS

For Education

Only two changes in practices need to be implemented to increase student achievement:

1. *Application to teaching of the specified instructional strategies shown by research to work.* Teaching the 20 instructional strategies in pre-service and in-service teacher education should not require additional time or money, provided that strategies shown by research not to work are eliminated. Teacher preparation programs tend to become bloated because more teaching practices are added over time than discontinued. Despite vested interests, it is important to eliminate common teaching practices proven by research not to increase academic achievement; for example, whole language instruction, ability grouping, and student reinforcement regimens.

2. *One-to-one tutoring.* It is feasible to begin preventive tutoring without incurring much additional cost. The special education teacher in charge of the resource room can supervise the preventive tutoring program and provide space and material for tutoring. Part-time peer and volunteer tutors can be recruited to provide almost all of the preventive tutoring needed. Some tutoring will continue to be done by the classroom teacher and by special education teachers. Since it is not feasible, moneywise and otherwise, to provide tutoring for all students in a school at first, preventive tutoring can begin in the primary grades and be added grade level by grade

level over time. One-to-one tutoring has proven to be very effective in preventing failure in the early grades where illiteracy is born. In addition, it alleviates the need to reduce class size.

Failure must be defined as failure to achieve grade-level learning objectives rather than failure to be promoted, since social promotion has become so prevalent and illiterates and undereducated students have been allowed to graduate.

Savings will accrue for the following reasons:

- Practices not proven to increase student achievement can be more readily distinguished and discontinued.

- An increase in student achievement would reduce the dropout and truancy rates, since dropouts usually fail and are truant before dropping out.

- A reduction in special education expenditure would be expected.

- Pressure for costly testing overkill, spurred nationally by accountability legislation, would abate when student achievement rises.

- The need for schools, including colleges, to offer remedial courses would be reduced.

For Society

It is important to realize that communities and businesses have pressed for accountability legislation because far too many students left school undereducated and illiterate. Illiterates tend to become social wards, drug addicts, and criminals, and only qualify for the most menial jobs. Educators, more often than not, try to impress the business world and their community with the accomplishments of star graduates, faculty achievements, and new buildings and equipment rather than with the reduction of academic failure. Failures tend to be labeled and dismissed as losers in America, but more have become wards than society can tolerate. Following are some of the savings of life and money educators could impress the business world and their community with by reducing student failure.

- More people would qualify for employment when they left school.

- Government employment agencies would not need to spend as much preparing the unemployed to find work.

- Less money would need to be spent by businesses for literacy education to qualify students for entry-level positions.

- Less money would need to be spent by government on drug rehabilitation, law enforcement, social work, criminal prosecution, and trials, as well as vocational training.

- Government would not need to spend as much for prisons, mental institutions, and homeless shelters.

HIGHLIGHTS

No magic is required to increase student achievement. Private enterprises such as Sylvan and Kaplan thrive, salvaging public school failures whose parents can afford their services. Some companies guarantee student success. Two changes in practice are needed:

1. Teacher preparation needs to focus on teaching the specified instructional strategies shown to increase academic achievement. If instructional practices shown not to increase academic achievement are excluded from teacher education, there should not be an increase in cost.

2. Additional one-to-one tutoring needs to be provided for students who fail class tests and assignments on particular topics. Present resources, including special education teachers, can be used as well as part-time volunteer tutors to keep costs at a minimum.

11

School Effectiveness Checklist

This checklist will help you to assess a school's effectiveness. It summarizes and highlights important attributes of effective schools.

Directions: Following are attributes of effective schools. Is the attribute described found in your school? Please circle either *Yes* or *No*. If you don't know, or aren't sure whether to circle *Yes* or *No* for any attribute, we have indicated the best source to turn to for information (P = Principal; S = Students).

Who to Ask	Attributes of Effective Schools	Circle One	
S	1. Classroom disruptions rarely interfere with teaching.	Yes	No
S	2. Prior to instruction, teachers specify to students the learning objectives the class is expected to achieve.	Yes	No
S	3. Teachers explain to students their plan for achieving learning objectives.	Yes	No
S	4. Teachers explain how students can tell when they have achieved learning objectives.	Yes	No
S	5. Students are placed in instructional programs where they are capable of succeeding.	Yes	No
P	6. Students are given books and materials they need to undertake assignments.	Yes	No
S	7. Students are given sufficient time to complete assignments.	Yes	No

Who to Ask	Attributes of Effective Schools	Circle One
P	8. Repetition is used to instill and solidify learning.	Yes No
S	9. Teacher presentations and instructions are clear and precise.	Yes No
S	10. Students are taught to use reminders to cue important information; for example, class notes, date books.	Yes No
S	11. Teachers keep students focused on the learning task.	Yes No
P	12. Aids are used to condense time and space when needed to clarify relationships; for example, maps, time-lapse photography, trips to the planetarium.	Yes No
P	13. Unifying schemes are used to teach relationships; for example, outlines, summaries, diagrams.	Yes No
S	14. Students are taught teamwork skills.	Yes No
S	15. Students are taught decision-making skills.	Yes No
P	16. Students are taught how to innovate.	Yes No
S	17. Teachers evaluate learning frequently.	Yes No
S	18. Students are given feedback on assignments and test results promptly.	Yes No
S	19. Needed corrective instruction is provided immediately after students are given feedback on assignments and tests.	Yes No
S	20. Teachers prepare students to complete their homework assignments on their own.	Yes No
P	21. Students are given all the one-on-one corrective instruction they need.	Yes No
S	22. Students' mistakes, test scores, and grades are fully explained to them.	Yes No
P	23. Classes contain students of different ability levels.	Yes No
S	24. Detailed procedures for deriving grades are explained to students and parents.	Yes No
S	25. Teachers spend 90 percent of class time teaching.	Yes No
P	26. Grades are assigned by comparing student performance with criteria of competent performance.	Yes No
S	27. Teachers use question-and-answer instruction frequently.	Yes No

Who to Ask	Attributes of Effective Schools	Circle One
P	28. Teachers know how to construct achievement tests to evaluate classroom instruction and learning.	Yes No
P	29. Parents can gain quick access to school administrators and teachers to discuss their child's deficient scores, grades, or conduct.	Yes No
P	30. Research-based in-service training is provided regularly to update teaching skills.	Yes No
P	31. Instructional techniques proven to be ineffective are not used; for example, whole language instruction and reinforcement.	Yes No
P	32. Teachers prepare written lesson plans prior to instruction.	Yes No
P	33. Teachers' lesson plans include alternative ways of teaching each topic.	Yes No
P	34. Teachers' instructional skills are evaluated in the classroom at least every three years.	Yes No
P	35. Students who fail year-end tests that certify achievement of grade-level objectives are not promoted or graduated.	Yes No
S	36. Student rules of conduct are specified and enforced.	Yes No
S	37. Teachers make an effort to interest students in the lessons they teach.	Yes No
S	38. Students are taught how to use prior knowledge to solve new problems.	Yes No
P	39. Teachers are hired based on their observed classroom teaching skills.	Yes No
S	40. After-school instruction is provided for students who need corrective instruction.	Yes No

Assessment Key:

- A school that scores 28 to 33 "Yes" (79% to 84%) of the attributes described is providing an adequate education for its students.
- A school that scores over 34 "Yes" (85%) of the attributes described is providing an excellent education for its students.

References

Anania, J. (1981). *The effects of quality of instruction on the cognitive and affective learning of students.* Unpublished doctoral dissertation, University of Chicago.

Block, J. H., & Anderson, L. W. (1975). *Mastery Learning in classroom instruction.* New York: Macmillan.

Bloom, B. S. (1964). *Stability and change in human characteristics.* New York: Wiley.

Bloom, B. S. (1968). Learning for mastery. *Evaluation Comment* (Ed. J. H. Block) *1*, 1–11.

Bloom, B. S. (1984, May). The search for methods of group instruction as effective as one-to-one tutoring. *Educational Leadership*, 4–17.

Bloom, B. S., & Peters, F. (1961). *Use of academic prediction scales for counseling and selecting college entrants.* Glencoe, IL: Free Press.

Burke, A. J. (1983). *Students' potential for learning contrasted under tutorial and group approaches to instruction.* Unpublished doctoral dissertation, University of Chicago.

Carnine, D. W. (1977). Phonics versus Look-Say: Transfer to new words. *The Reading Teacher 30*, 636–639.

Carroll, J. (1968). A model of school learning. *Teacher's College Record 64*, 723–733.

Centers for Disease Control. (1992). *The prevention of youth violence: A framework for community action.* Atlanta: Division of Injury Control.

Evertson, C. M. (1995). *Classroom organization and management program.* Revalidation submission to the Program Effectiveness Panel, Department of Education.

Frankel, J. R., & Wallen, N. E. (1996). *How to design and evaluate research in education.* New York: McGraw-Hill.

Friedman, M. I. (2000). *Ensuring student success.* Columbia, SC: Institute for Evidence-Based Decision-Making in Education.

Friedman, M. I., & Fisher, S. P. (1998). *Handbook on effective instructional strategies.* Columbia, SC: Institute for Evidence-Based Decision-Making in Education.

Friedman, M. I. et al. (2003). *Educators' handbook on effective testing.* Columbia, SC: Institute for Evidence-Based Decision-Making in Education.

Gettinger, M. (1984). Achievement as a function of time spent learning and time needed for learning. *American Educational Research Journal 21*(3), 617–628.

Hammill, D. D., Brown, L., & Bryant, B. R. (1992). *A consumer's guide to tests in print* (2nd ed.). Austin, TX: PRO-ED.

Hong, H. (1996). Effects of mathematics learning through children's literature on math achievement and dispositional outcomes. *Early Childhood Research Quarterly 11*, 477–494.

McLoughlin, J. A., & Lewis, R. B. (2001). *Assessing students with special needs.* Upper Saddle River, NJ: Merrill/Prentice Hall.

National Commission on Excellence in Education, U.S. Department of Education. (1983). *A nation at risk.* Washington, DC: Author.

Rickel, A. U., & Fields, R. B. (1983). Storybook models and achievement behavior of pre-school children. *Psychology in the Schools 20*, 105–112.

Rosier, M. J., & Keeves, J. P. (1991). *The IEA study of science I: Science education and curricula in twenty-three countries.* Vol. 8 of *International Studies in Education Achievement.* New York: Pergamon Press.

Salvia, J., & Ysseldyke, J. E. (2001). *Assessment* (8th ed.). Boston: Houghton Mifflin.

Slavin, R. E., Madden, M. A., Dolan, L. J., & Wasik, B. A. (1996). *Every child, every school: Success for all.* Thousand Oaks, CA: Sage Publications.

Slavin, R. E., Madden, M. A., & Leavey, M. B. (1984). Effects of team assisted individualization on the mathematics achievement of academically handicapped students and nonhandicapped students. *Journal of Educational Psychology 76*, 813–819.

Sweetland, R. C., & Keyser, D. J. (1991). *Tests: A comprehensive reference for assessments in psychology, education, and business* (3rd ed.). Austin, TX: PRO-ED.

Toyama, N., Lee, Y. M., & Muto, T. (1997). Japanese preschoolers' understanding of biological concepts related to procedures for animal care. *Early Childhood Research Quarterly 12*, 347–360.

U.S. Department of Health, Education, and Welfare. (1978). *Violent schools, safe schools: The safe schools report to Congress.* Washington, DC: Author.

Wittrock, M. C. (Ed.). (1986). *Handbook of research on teaching.* New York: Macmillan.

Wolff, P. (1972). The role of stimulus-correlated activity in children's recognition of nonsense forms. *Journal of Experimental Child Psychology 14*, 427–441.

Index